SOCIETY FOR OLD TESTAMENT STUDY
MONOGRAPH SERIES

GENERAL EDITOR
R. E. CLEMENTS

5

THE WAY OF THE WILDERNESS

A GEOGRAPHICAL STUDY OF
THE WILDERNESS ITINERARIES IN THE OLD TESTAMENT

THE WAY OF
THE WILDERNESS

A GEOGRAPHICAL STUDY OF
THE WILDERNESS ITINERARIES
IN THE OLD TESTAMENT

G. I. DAVIES

*Lecturer in Theology at the
University of Nottingham*

CAMBRIDGE UNIVERSITY PRESS

CAMBRIDGE

LONDON · NEW YORK · MELBOURNE

Published by the Syndics of the Cambridge University Press
The Pitt Building, Trumpington Street, Cambridge CB2 1RP
Bentley House, 200 Euston Road, London NW1 2DB
32 East 57th Street, New York, NY 10022, USA
296 Beaconsfield Parade, Middle Park, Melbourne 3206, Australia

© Cambridge University Press 1979

First published 1979

Printed in Great Britain at the
University Press, Cambridge

Library of Congress Cataloguing in Publication Data

Davies, G. I.
The way of the wilderness.

(Monograph series – Society for Old Testament Study; 5)
Bibliography: p.
Includes index.
1. Exodus, The – Biblical teaching. 2. Bible. O.T. Exodus – Geography.
3. Bible. O.T. Exodus – Criticism, interpretation, etc. – History. I. Title.
II. Series: Society for Old Testament Study. Monograph series; 5.
BS 680.E9D38   222'.9'5   77-95442

ISBN 0 521 22057 2

CONTENTS

PREFACE

This monograph is a revised version of Part II of my doctoral dissertation submitted to the University of Cambridge in 1975. During the writing of it I have been aware of my indebtedness to many teachers and friends for their insights and, not least, their questions. I should like to record my thanks in particular to the following: to Dr R. E. Clements (who supervised my research and, as Editor, accepted this work for the Monograph Series), Dr S. P. Brock and Dr C. J. Labuschagne, all of whom read the original manuscript and made many helpful suggestions; to Professor J. A. Emerton, whose rigorous handling of exegetical and other problems has been a source of inspiration throughout my work; to Dr P. S. Alexander and Dr Z. Meshel, who advised me on particular points; to the Society for Old Testament Study and the Managers of the Hort Fund of the University of Cambridge, for generous contributions to the cost of publication; and to the staff of the Cambridge University Press, for their exceptionally careful and courteous handling of the process of production.

The transcription of place-names is a familiar problem to workers in this field, and I have adopted the following policy here. Where there is a well-known English form, as with Biblical names, I have used this; where there is not, I have reproduced the name in an Anglicised form which keeps as close as possible to the original, without, generally, employing the diacritical marks that would be needed for absolute precision. With the help of the maps there should be no difficulty in establishing what site is meant, and specialists will know where to find the exact spelling. I dedicate this work to my parents, in gratitude for the opportunities and encouragement which they have so freely given me.

University of Nottingham G.I.D.
October 1978

ABBREVIATIONS

AJ	*Antiquitates Judaicae* (Josephus)
ANET	*Ancient Near Eastern Texts Relating to the Old Testament*, ed. J. B. Pritchard (Princeton, 1950: 2nd edn 1955; 3rd edn 1969)
AUSS	*Andrews University Seminary Studies*
BA	*Biblical Archaeologist*
BASOR	*Bulletin of the American Schools of Oriental Research*
BDB	F. Brown, S. R. Driver and C. A. Briggs, *A Hebrew and English Lexicon of the Old Testament* (Oxford, 1906)
BH³	*Biblia Hebraica*, 3rd edn ed. R. Kittel, A. Alt and O. Eissfeldt (Stuttgart, 1937)
BHS	*Biblia Hebraica Stuttgartensia*, ed. K. Elliger and W. Rudolph (Stuttgart, 1968–)
BIE	*Bulletin de l'Institut d'Égypte*
BIFAO	*Bulletin de l'Institut Français d'Archéologie Orientale*
BZAW	*Beiheft zur Zeitschrift für die Alttestamentliche Wissenschaft*
CBQ	*Catholic Biblical Quarterly*
CCSL	*Corpus Christianorum, Series Latina*
CSCO	*Corpus Scriptorum Christianorum Orientalium*
CSEL	*Corpus Scriptorum Ecclesiasticorum Latinorum*
DBS	*Dictionnaire de la Bible, Supplément*, ed. L. Pirot *et al.* (Paris, 1928–)
DLZ	*Deutsche Literaturzeitung*
ET	English translation
GGM	*Geographici Graeci Minores*, ed. C. Müller (Paris, 1855–61)
GTTOT	J. Simons, *The Geographical and Topographical Texts of the Old Testament* (Leiden, 1959)
HTR	*Harvard Theological Review*
HUCA	*Hebrew Union College Annual*
ICC	*International Critical Commentary*

IDB	*The Interpreter's Dictionary of the Bible*, ed. G. A. Buttrick *et al.* (Nashville and New York, 1962)
IDB(S)	*The Interpreter's Dictionary of the Bible, Supplementary Volume*, ed. K. Crim *et al.* (Nashville, 1976)
IEJ	*Israel Exploration Journal*
IOSCS	*International Organisation for Septuagint and Cognate Studies*
JAOS	*Journal of the American Oriental Society*
JBL	*Journal of Biblical Literature*
JEA	*Journal of Egyptian Archaeology*
JNES	*Journal of Near Eastern Studies*
JPOS	*Journal of the Palestine Oriental Society*
JSS	*Journal of Semitic Studies*
JTS	*Journal of Theological Studies*
KAI	*Kanaanäische und Aramäische Inschriften*, ed. H. Donner and W. Röllig (Wiesbaden, 1962–4)
LSJ	H. G. Liddell and R. Scott, *A Greek–English Lexicon*, 9th edn revised by H. S. Jones (Oxford, 1940)
LXX	Septuagint Version
MT	Masoretic Text
P	Priestly Work
PEFQS	*Palestine Exploration Fund Quarterly Statement*
PEQ	*Palestine Exploration Quarterly*
PG	*Patrologia Graeca* (ed. J.-P. Migne)
PJB	*Palästinajahrbuch*
PL	*Patrologia Latina* (ed. J.-P. Migne)
RB	*Revue Biblique*
RE	Pauly–Wissowa–Kroll, *Realencyclopaedie der Klassischen Altertumswissenschaft*
Sam.	Samaritan Pentateuch
SBL	Society of Biblical Literature
SC	*Sources Chrétiennes*
SVT	*Supplement to Vetus Testamentum*
TB	*Tyndale Bulletin*
TLZ	*Theologische Literaturzeitung*
VetChr	*Vetera Christianorum*
VT	*Vetus Testamentum*
ZDPV	*Zeitschrift der Deutschen Palästinavereins*

MAPS

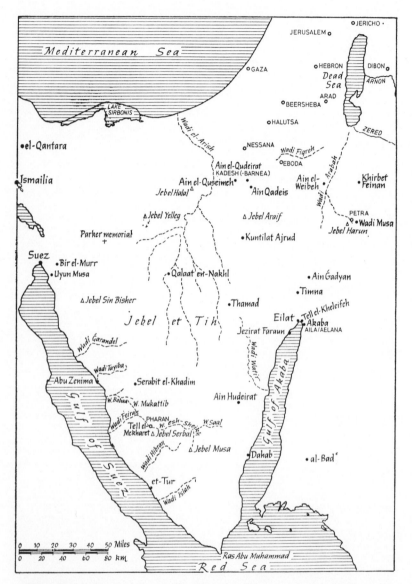

1   The Sinai Peninsula and adjacent areas. (*Ancient names are in capitals.*)

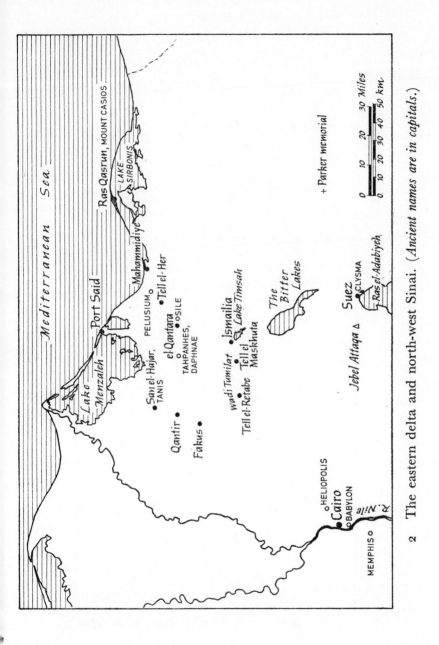

2   The eastern delta and north-west Sinai. (*Ancient names are in capitals.*)

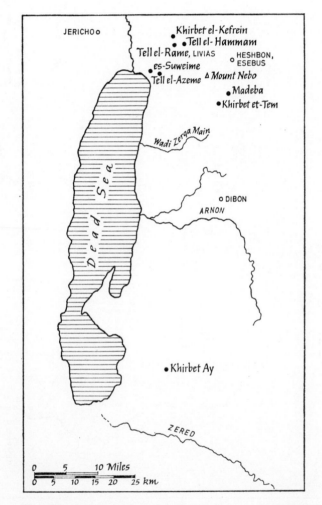

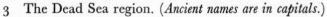

3   The Dead Sea region. (*Ancient names are in capitals.*)

CHAPTER I

INTRODUCTION

Among the geographical texts in the Pentateuch the wilderness itineraries form a group which provide especially precise information and share an unusually similar structure.[1] The longest and most complete example is found in Num. 33: 1–49, but parallels to parts of this passage exist in a series of isolated verses in the main narrative of Exodus and Numbers, which show agreement with it in content and structure, and often in verbal details as well (e.g. Ex. 12: 37a).[2] Shorter itineraries are to be found in Num. 21: 12–20 and Dt. 10: 6–7. These passages belong, from the point of view of their form, to a widely attested literary genre of the ancient world, which survives mainly in official documents. It is probable that this way of presenting a route was borrowed by the writers of the Old Testament from the repertoire of the archives of the Israelite royal court.

In view of their primary function – which is to describe routes – it is only to be expected that the geographical significance of the wilderness itineraries would be a topic of continuing interest to readers and interpreters of the books in which they occur. It is certainly this aspect of the texts which has received the greatest attention from scholars in the modern period, to the neglect, it must be said, of other features such as their formal characteristics. Even in earlier periods there were powerful forces which, in differing degrees in different situations, provided a stimulus for the geographical approach. The existence of a developed topographical science in both classical antiquity and among the medieval Arabs contributed a framework and an environment in which it was natural for the identification of places mentioned in the Bible to be attempted. Again, the popularity of pilgrimages to the Holy Land and neighbouring areas from the fourth century AD onwards encouraged an interest in such questions within Christian circles, and it is certainly to this practice of pilgrimage that we owe the preservation at least of a great deal of traditional material bearing on our subject.[3] In Rabbinic Judaism a further factor required a geographical approach to some texts: the need, for halakhic purposes, to define the limits of 'the land of Israel'.[4]

At the same time it would be wrong to suppose that the topographical approach to the itineraries was dominant in early Jewish and Christian interpretation. There was, at least from the time of Philo onwards, an influential tradition of 'spiritual interpretation', which was more concerned with the amplification of what happened at the places named and with the treatment of this as a symbol of spiritual reality than with their identification in terms of current geographical knowledge. The Biblical commentaries used by both Jews and Christians until quite modern times contained only matter directed towards this edifying treatment of the texts, and are consequently of little immediate interest for our present inquiry. They would however provide plentiful material for a quite separate examination of the role played by the itineraries in Jewish and Christian spirituality.[5]

It is nevertheless with geography that we are concerned here. In previous treatments of the wilderness itineraries two lines of inquiry have generally and understandably been interwoven.[6] To what routes, on the one hand, have the itineraries traditionally been thought to refer? On the other hand, to which routes were they originally intended to refer? We propose to keep these two approaches to the texts apart in the first instance. By doing this we hope to do more justice than is usually done to the history of the tradition (or rather, traditions) of interpretation as a subject in its own right; and also to avoid the common tendency to overlook the presuppositions on which individual identifications in the tradition are based. It is only when the tradition and its own processes of development have been investigated that its value for a modern historical (or historico-geographical) inquiry can be adequately assessed.

One problem that quickly emerges in connection with the tradition is the paucity of material that is available for the most ancient period. This might simply be due to the selection of certain traditions (from a more abundant corpus) by the writers of the works that happen to survive. But probably it points to a situation in which a complete series of identifications had not yet been arrived at. Even the *Onomasticon* of Eusebius (on which see further below, pp. 30–7), which apparently gives as much topographical information as he could discover, frequently says no more about places in the wilderness than σταθμὸς τῶν υἱῶν Ἰσραὴλ ἐπὶ τῆς ἐρήμου. Whatever the reason, we are often not in a position to cite as much information as we should like. In what follows it will be necessary to mention more general indications of where the Israelites were thought to have travelled, which are not always directly related to the itineraries themselves. This should not be misleading, since until modern times it was generally held that all the data in Exodus and Numbers referred to the same route (hence the need felt for the harmonisations found at some points in the Samaritan Pentateuch, the LXX and the Targumim). An interpretation of the route based on non-itinerary material will still indicate the background against which the itineraries were being read and understood.

CHAPTER 2

JEWISH INTERPRETATIONS IN GREEK

The Jewish material may for convenience be divided into two parts according to the language in which it was written: Greek in the one case, Hebrew or Aramaic in the other. An important corollary of this linguistic division is the use by the one group of Greek versions of the Old Testament, while the other group works primarily from the Hebrew text. The division according to language also corresponds to a chronological division, as the Greek material dates chiefly from before 100 AD, while the Hebrew and Aramaic texts are later, although they may contain traditions which originated before this date. Although we adopt this division of the material, we do not imply that there is no contact between the two groups of texts. In fact our study confirms that at certain points there is indeed contact between them.[1]

THE SEPTUAGINT

Only occasionally does the LXX itself indicate the direction in which the Israelites were thought to have gone. Most of the Hebrew names are simply transliterated or (occasionally) translated, and variations from MT can be explained by textual corruption in either the Hebrew or the Greek stage of transmission. It is possible that in some cases the LXX preserves the names more accurately than does MT. At one point (Num. 33: 36) the fuller text of most LXX witnesses must be attributed to a secondary harmonisation of the passage to make it agree with a statement earlier in the narrative (Num. 13: 26 (LXX v. 27)). The renderings of itinerary-material which show an interest in geographical interpretation all relate to Egypt or its borders, and serve to locate the starting-point of the journey, the encampment by 'the sea' and the actual sea that was crossed.

Rameses itself is not given a Greek equivalent, but it is vocalised in such a way as to approximate more closely in LXX than in MT to the Egyptian pronunciation. But in Gen. 45–7 (cf. especially 47: 11) 'the land of Rameses' occurs as an alternative description to 'the land of Goshen' for the area occupied by Jacob and his family. (In fact in Gen. 46: 28 LXX has εἰς γῆν Ραμεσση corresponding to the ארצה גשן of MT). The identification of Goshen does seem to have been a concern of the translator. In two verses where MT has בארץ גשן LXX interprets with ἐν γῇ Γεσεμ ᾽Αραβίας/-ίᾳ (Gen. 45: 10; 46: 34). ᾽Αραβία is here not used to refer to Arabia proper but to a region in the north-east of Egypt, either the 'Arabian' nome itself (nome XX) or a wider area corresponding more or less to the whole isthmus of Suez.[2] Apparently Goshen is regarded by the translator as equivalent to either a part or the whole of one of these areas. In two other passages of Genesis (46: 28, 29) גשן (in fact with the directional suffix ה-) appears without ארץ, and here the translator took it to be the name of a city and rendered it by the name of Hellenistic Heroopolis, which epigraphic evidence shows to have been located at or near Tell el-Maskhuta in Wadi Tumilat.[3] Thus the area occupied by the Israelites before the Exodus is fixed by the use of contemporary geographical terms as being around this site and Rameses was presumably thought to be nearby.[4] As will appear, later tradition knew of more exact locations than this for the starting-point of the journey.

The encampment by the sea is located by reference to three places, Pi-hahiroth, Migdol and Baal-zephon (Ex. 14: 2, 9; Num. 33: 7). The LXX translator of Exodus gave as the equivalent for Pi-hahiroth ἡ ἔπαυλις, which means according to LSJ (1) 'steading' (2), 'farm-building', (3) '(military) quarters', (4) 'unwalled village'. Elsewhere in the LXX the word is used chiefly of unprotected settlements and is most often equivalent to Hebrew חצר.[5] It is difficult to regard it as a translation of the name 'Pi-hahiroth', and the apparatuses of BH³ and BHS suggest that instead of החירת the Vorlage of LXX may have had חצרת. There are several difficulties with this view, not

5

the least being that the translator seems only to have translated Hebrew names when this was necessary to bring out a play on words in the Hebrew, as in 15: 23 and 17: 7. It is more likely that he was referring to a contemporary tradition which identified Pi-hahiroth with a place called in Greek Ἡ Ἔπαυλις. Though it might seem improbable for such a word to be used as a proper name, there is evidence of just such a use of it in papyri.[6] Unfortunately the location of the place can no longer be established with certainty. But Etheria mentions a place called Epauleum near Clysma (*Peregrinatio* 7.4), which was apparently equated with Pi-hahiroth in the fourth century AD, and it is possible that this is the place to which LXX referred.[7]

It has become a commonplace of modern Biblical scholarship that the Hebrew ים סוף does not *mean* 'the Red Sea' but 'the sea of reeds'.[8] It has consequently been questioned whether 'the sea' of the book of Exodus was the Red Sea (i.e. the Gulf of Suez) after all. The LXX translator is quite clear in his belief that it was, since in his version ἡ ἐρυθρὰ θάλασσα is the regular equivalent to ים סוף (cf. Ex. 13: 18; 15: 4, 22). Since there is no evidence of this name having been used of the Mediterranean Sea or the northern lakes in ancient times, however vague popular views of its southerly and easterly extent may have been, there can be no doubt that LXX located the deliverance at the sea to the south of the isthmus of Suez, presumably in what is known now as the Gulf of Suez.

PHILO

The voluminous writings of Philo Judaeus do little to amplify this meagre evidence of an Alexandrian tradition of geographical interpretation. Philo was of course primarily interested in the Old Testament for its didactic and symbolic value. He uses 'Heroopolis' for גשן in the place corresponding to Gen. 46: 28–9 (*De Jos.* 256) and he regularly represents ים סוף by ἡ ἐρυθρὰ θάλασσα (*De Vita Mos.* 1.165, etc.). These equations are obviously due to the fact that the LXX was Philo's Bible. He speaks of the beginning of the Israelites' route as not the straight road, which would have brought them into Canaan in three days (?) but one at an angle to it (ibid. 1.163–5), which he later describes as a long road through the desert not normally used (ibid. 2.247). This is little more than intelligent amplification of Ex. 13: 17–18.

The only point at which Philo's exegesis presupposes further research is in the location of the battle with Amalek (Ex. 17: 8–13) close to the borders of the land to be occupied by Israel, 'which was then occupied by Phoenicians' (ibid. 2.214ff). The general idea that the Amalekites lived on the borders of Canaan could have been deduced from a number of Old Testament passages (e.g. 1 Sam. 27: 8) but it is remarkable to find 'Phoenicians' mentioned, as they lived much further to the north than any place which Philo can have had in mind. In fact it is Philo's utter dependence on LXX which can be shown to be responsible. In Ex. 16: 35, immediately before the narration of the two Rephidim incidents, it is said that Israel 'ate the manna, till they came to the border of the land of Canaan'. For the last clause LXX has:

ἕως παρεγένοντο εἰς μέρος τῆς Φοινίκης.

The use of Φοινίκη for the כנען of MT is unusual though not quite unparalleled.[9] Philo evidently thought that the manna was eaten only as far as the next stopping-place after the Wilderness of Sin to be mentioned, i.e. Rephidim, and that it was this which was in 'Phoenicia'.

JOSEPHUS

Josephus, as a historian, not surprisingly displays more interest than Philo in the Israelites' route. In fact he gives rather different versions of the beginning of the route in the *Antiquities* and in the *Contra Apionem*, but in view of the apologetic character of the latter work we may confidently regard the account in the *Antiquities* as containing the results of Josephus' own research into the Biblical text and local traditions. The *Contra Apionem* is however of considerable interest for the light which it sheds on other contemporary views of the route of the Exodus, and cannot be ignored here.

Josephus is not dependent on LXX to the extent that Philo is. There are many places where he has a different transcription of a proper name from LXX, and occasionally he offers an improved translation of MT.[10] At the same time his transcriptions sometimes agree with LXX against MT, and he interprets 'Goshen' in Gen. 46: 28–9 as the ancient name of Heroopolis, just like LXX.[11] This may seem to justify the view that Josephus had direct access to the Hebrew text but also referred to LXX.[12] But the 'improvements' on LXX may be due not to Josephus making his own Greek translation but to the use of the revisions of LXX which recent textual study has shown to have been in existence already in the first century AD.[13] Indeed it has long been recognised that in the later books of the Old Testament, where the evidence is clearer, Josephus often shows knowledge of readings which diverge from the unrevised LXX and appear later in manuscripts affected by the Lucianic recension. The fact that this is not so clear in the Pentateuch may be due to the fact that the evidence of the revisions of LXX is much sparser there.[14]

The point from which, according to Josephus, the itinerary begins is indirectly indicated by what he says about the settlement of Jacob and his family in Egypt. According to AJ 2.188 this was 'in Heliopolis'. This apparently represents a different tradition from that known to LXX, though it is interesting to observe that LXX too introduces Heliopolis into the Exodus account, against MT, in the list of 'store-cities' in Ex. 1: 11.[15] While it may well be correct to recognise the influence of a Jewish community in Heliopolis in these innovations, a Biblical basis for at least Josephus' reference to Heliopolis could be found in Gen. 45: 10, where Joseph says that his family shall be 'near' him, and Gen. 41: 50–2, which could be taken as implying that Joseph's home was at On, known in Hellenistic times as Heliopolis. A starting-point for the journey at a place close to modern Cairo, like the site of Heliopolis, is essential if the rest of Josephus' interpretation of the beginning of the route is to be intelligible.

Josephus relates that Israel went by way of Letopolis, which was not occupied at the time of the Exodus (AJ 2.315). He appears from what he says about it to have held that Letopolis was the same place as the Babylon built in the time of Cambyses of Persia. This lay on the eastern bank of the Nile about 10 miles (16 km) south of Heliopolis. From here the Israelites are supposed to have gone by a short cut (συντόμως) to the Red Sea, reaching it on the third day, as the Biblical account suggests if each stage is taken to last just one day. The route taken seems to have led south of Jebel Attaqa and to have reached the sea south-west of Ras el-Adabiyeh. The journey via Letopolis/ Babylon would have involved a quite pointless detour to the south if it were eventually intended to take a more northerly route; and only the view adopted here makes sense of Josephus' very circumstantial account of the events leading up to the crossing of the sea (AJ 2.324–5). The passage is of sufficient interest to be quoted in full:

τὰς δὲ ὁδοὺς ἀπεφράγνυσαν [sc. the Egyptians], αἷς φεύξεσθαι τοὺς Ἑβραίους ὑπελάμβανον, μεταξὺ κρημνῶν αὐτοὺς ἀπροσβάτων καὶ τῆς θαλάττης ἀπολαμβάνοντες· τελευτᾷ γὰρ εἰς αὐτὴν ὄρος ὑπὸ τραχύτητος ὁδῶν ἄπορον καὶ φυγῆς ἀπολαμβανόμενον. τοιγαροῦν ἐν τῇ εἰσβολῇ τῇ πρὸς θάλατταν τοῦ ὄρους τοὺς Ἑβραίους ἀπέφραττον τῷ στρατοπέδῳ κατὰ στόμα τοῦτο ἱδρυσάμενοι, ὅπως τὴν εἰς τὸ πεδίον ἔξοδον ὦσιν αὐτοὺς ἀφῃρημένοι.

The Israelites were trapped between a mountain and the sea, where there was only a narrow passable strip of land, which they would have to traverse to get safely away, to the πεδίον. The Egyptians overtook them and blocked this way of escape with their army. In several respects this description goes far beyond what is narrated in Ex. 14, not least in the introduction of the all-important mountain. There is no need now to try to establish how this expansion of the Exodus narrative arose, although it may be significant that certain Rabbinic explanations of the name Pi-hahiroth imply that it was a place close to a mountainous region. The only place by the Red Sea that really comes into consideration is where Jebel Attaqa terminates in the promontory of Ras el-Adabiyeh. If this is the right place, then the nature of the Egyptians' strategy demands that the Israelites be on the south side of the promontory, hoping apparently to make their way around the north end of the Gulf of Suez. If they were approaching the seaward end of Jebel Attaqa from the north they would be aiming in quite the wrong direction.

After crossing the 'Red Sea' the Israelites made for Mount Sinai (*AJ* 3.1). Josephus does not give such a precise account of this part of the route – which may mean that this was not such a great concern of contemporary tradition as the location of places connected with the Exodus itself. What he does say can be, and has been, taken as evidence that he knew nothing of the tradition that Mount Sinai was in the south of the Sinai peninsula. The main points are his association of the Amalekites who appear at Rephidim, the stopping-place before Sinai, with Petra and Gobolitis (*AJ* 3.40 – cf. 2.6); and the representation of the 'Midian' to which Moses fled as a city on or near to the Red Sea (*AJ* 2.256–7), by which he probably meant one of the places of that name located by Ptolemy in north-west Arabia (*Geography* 6.7.2, 27). In addition the name 'Paran', which later was identified with the place Faran in the south of the Sinai peninsula, is simply given a Hellenised form by Josephus (Φάραγξ, meaning 'a ravine') and said to be close to Canaan (*AJ* 3.300), as the Biblical narrative would suggest.

It has therefore been suggested that for Josephus Mount Sinai was in north-west Arabia.[16] There is an obstacle to this theory in the one statement about the location of Mount Sinai itself which Josephus does make: he says that it is 'between Egypt and Arabia' (*Contra Apionem* 2.25). This is difficult to reconcile with its being in Arabia proper. It suggests that Josephus had a more westerly area in mind, in fact what is now known as the Sinai peninsula. The description of Mount Sinai which he gives in *AJ* 3.76 suggests that he knew of a particular peak which was identified with Sinai. But where in the peninsula was it? The statements about the Amalekites and Midian quoted above would be most compatible with a tradition which located Mount Sinai somewhere in the north-east of the peninsula, perhaps as far north as Jebel Araif. But to argue from them is to assume that Josephus had carefully coordinated the various geographical comments which he makes about the central part of the wilderness journey, and it is not at all clear that he did so. If he merely brought together such evidence as he could muster for the location and nature of the places mentioned in the Biblical narratives, without going into the question of a route connecting them together – and this may very well be what he did – then it remains a possibility that his description of Mount Sinai refers to a peak elsewhere in the peninsula, possibly even in the south.[17]

The later part of the route is no easier to trace in detail, but an important landmark is the placing of Mount Hor, where Aaron died, at Petra, the Arab (i.e. Nabataean) metropolis formerly known as Arcē according to Josephus (AJ 4.82).[18] This suggests that the preceding episodes, such as the refusal of the king of Idumaea (*sic*) to permit a passage through his territory (4.76–7) and the death of Miriam at Mount (*sic*)[19] Zin (4.78–81), were thought of as taking place in the southern Negeb, as a march through the desert comes between them and the arrival at Petra. Kadesh is not mentioned by Josephus at all, and it must remain uncertain whether the Targumic tradition that it was at Petra too was current when he wrote. From Petra the route must have been envisaged as taking an eventual northerly direction to the Arnon, which Josephus speaks of as a river flowing into the Dead Sea from the east and forming the boundary between Moabite and Amorite territory (AJ 4.85 – cf. Num. 21: 13). Josephus says nothing of any southerly journey from Petra, passing over Num. 21: 4 which would seem to suggest this. The final encampment is located opposite Jericho (AJ 4.100), and Moses delivers his final speech before his death where the city of Abila stood in Josephus' time (4.176). The latter may have been deduced from the reference to Abel-shittim in connection with the final encampment in Num. 33:49. According to Josephus Abila was 60 stades from the river Jordan (AJ 5.4): in modern times it has been located at Khirbet el-Kefrein, about 7 miles (11.2 km) from the northern end of the Dead Sea.[20]

A complete route for the wilderness journey cannot be

reconstructed from the data which Josephus provides, but his account shows that already by the end of the first century AD some places on it had been identified. We have seen this to be the case with at least the crossing of the sea, the location of Mount Sinai, the place of Aaron's death and the place where Moses delivered his final speech. Since some of these places were in outlying areas, it is probable that already at this time special visits to them ('pilgrimages') were made by Jews and that one of Josephus' sources for his account of the wilderness journey was their reports.[21]

In *Contra Apionem* Josephus discusses the Exodus at two different points in his argument. First, by identifying the Israelites with the Hyksos mentioned by Manetho, the Egyptian chronicler who wrote about 300 BC, he seeks to prove the antiquity of the Jewish people (*Contra Apionem* 1.73–105). Then, later in the work (ibid. 1.227–2.32), he deals with various non-Jewish accounts of the Exodus, including one attributed to Manetho,[22] only to repudiate them as malicious fictions.

According to Manetho, the Hyksos king Salitis built a fortress at a place called Avaris, where he used to go each summer, described as ἐν νομῷ τῷ Σεθροΐτη πόλιν ἐπικαιροτάτην, κειμένην μὲν πρὸς ἀνατολὴν τοῦ Βουβαστίτου ποταμοῦ (ibid. 1.78). He goes on to relate how, prior to their eventual expulsion, the Hyksos were confined in Avaris and eventually left there under a treaty for Syria (ibid. 1.86, 89). The location of Avaris is still a debated question,[23] but there is some reason for thinking that Josephus located it at Pelusium, on the Mediterranean coast. When discussing a second story of Manetho's, in which Avaris is again mentioned as a centre of opposition to a Pharaoh (ibid. 1.238, 241), Josephus says that the Egyptian king 'marched to Pelusium' to meet the rebels (ch. 274). Thus, if these stories are taken together, it seems that a very northerly point of departure for the Hyksos, and therefore, in Josephus' terms, for the Israelites, is being envisaged.

How this idea was to be reconciled with the tradition of a more southerly settlement and route found in the *Antiquities* Josephus does not tell us. But it seems that Josephus' advocacy of a northern point of departure here was not simply a result of his apologetically motivated identification of the Israelites with the Hyksos. He was in fact following an alternative tradition which can be traced back some fifty years before he wrote. Both the story of the Exodus attributed to Manetho (which may be a (first century AD?) supplement or adaptation of a story that did not refer to the Jews at all) and that of Chaeremon, Nero's tutor (*Contra Apionem* 1.288–303, especially 291), associate the Exodus with Pelusium. Although it is only attested at this time in pagan writers, it is quite likely that this was in origin a Jewish tradition. The identification of Rameses with Pelusium is the normal one in the Palestinian Targum (below, pp. 19, 21). Where on this view the route went after Pelusium can only be conjectured. It would be natural to suppose that the coast road to Palestine was followed, and this may have been the pagan understanding of it. But for a Jew like Josephus, who knew the significance of Ex. 13: 17–18 (cf. *AJ* 2.322–3) and accepted the LXX tradition of the equivalence of Yam Suf to the Gulf of Suez, this alternative would be excluded.[24]

CHAPTER 3

JEWISH INTERPRETATIONS IN HEBREW AND ARAMAIC

At first glance the Hebrew and Aramaic texts appear to be unpromising material for a geographical inquiry such as this. Where there is any interest at all in the itineraries and the names that appear in them, the approach is generally that of the etymologising midrash. This kind of interpretation, which could find some justification in the Old Testament itself (cf. Ex. 17: 7; Num. 11: 3, 34), deduces from a name something about the early history of Israel, assuming that the name was conferred on the place because of a specific occurrence in Israel's past. Even where this kind of exegesis is not present, the overall interest of the translators and commentators seems to be in non-geographical aspects of the Biblical text, either the harmonising of apparently contradictory accounts or the extracting of a universal halakhic principle from it. Yet such 'spiritualising' interpretations are not the whole of what these exegetes had to say about the text.[1] There are some indications of an interest in geographical questions in the treatment of the itineraries. Unfortunately this most often happens in the Targumim, where the identifications are anonymous and there is often no sure way of distinguishing an early interpretation from a comparatively late one. In a few cases, where a tradition is attested elsewhere, it is possible to affirm that it originated in or before the Tannaitic period, for example.[2]

Even where this is not possible, the fact that the Jews of the Tannaitic period were interested in the location of places mentioned in the itineraries shows that the traditions of identification may come from quite early Rabbinic Judaism. Thus in B. Ber. 54a (a baraitha) a list of places at which a Jew must give 'thanksgiving and praise to the Almighty' includes 'the place of the crossing of the Red Sea', 'the fords of the Jordan', 'the stone on which Moses sat when Joshua fought with Amalek' and 'the fords of the streams of Arnon'. This looks like a list of places that might be visited on a pilgrimage.[3] In addition the tales of Rabbah b. bar Hana, a third-century rabbi, show the appeal of the holy places to Jews, even though they cannot be regarded as having direct biographical value.[4] The rabbi told how he had been guided by an Arab merchant to places in the desert which were said to be the sites of events which took place on the wilderness journey. He claimed to have seen the bodies of those who died in the wilderness (cf. Num. 14: 32), then Mount Sinai, and then two smoking fissures in the ground, into which, according to his guide, 'the men of Korah' fell (B. Bab. Bathr. 74a). Two other Talmudic passages (and Rashi on Num. 33: 49) make use of a report by Rabbah b. bar Hana that he had visited the site of the final encampment in Transjordan, 'from Beth-jeshimoth as far as Abel-shittim', and that it measured three parasangs by three (B. Erub. 55b, Yoma 75b).

There is also, perhaps, some epigraphic evidence of Jewish pilgrimages. The Nabataean inscriptions of the Sinai peninsula are well known. But recent exploration has shown that there are also a number of ancient Hebrew inscriptions in the area, often accompanied by drawings of the menorah.[5] The circumstances in which these inscriptions came to be written is not made clear by their contents, but it is certainly attractive to associate them with journeys by Jews to sacred sites in the peninsula. Even if that were not the primary purpose of their visits, the Hebrew inscriptions and menoroth will remain important evidence for Jewish travel in the Sinai peninsula, where, not very much later, Christians were to find the sites of many of the wilderness events. In the light of this, and the evidence noted in the previous paragraph, the view that the Christians to a large extent took over identifications already made by Jews has some *a priori* probability.

There are various ways in which the geographical material in Rabbinic sources might be presented. One might consider together the interpretations offered by all the texts available, progressing through the itinerary in order as we have done, for example, in the case of Josephus. But this would not make clear the varying extent of relevant material in the different texts. Another possible approach would be to treat the traditions chronologically, beginning with those which can be shown to have originated in the Tannaitic period or before and showing how the corpus of tradition accumulated. In theory this is the most desirable approach, but it could only be applied to a limited extent, as in a great many cases we just do not know how old a particular tradition of identification is. As in other respects so in this the Targumim are the result of a long process of the amplification and revision of tradition, which remains obscure at many points.

We have therefore adopted an approach which makes no claims to show the gradual development of the tradition (although we shall of course discuss the antiquity and also the basis of traditions where possible), but which will make clear how the different texts which survive vary in the degree to which they attempt to fix contemporary equivalents for Biblical place-names. We shall take each Targum separately, beginning with that which has the least interpretative matter – the Peshitta[6] – and progressing to the fullest text, the Targum of Pseudo-Jonathan (Targum Yerushalmi I) by way of those which occupy an intermediate position, the Targum of Onkelos and Targum Yerushalmi II, represented primarily by the Neofiti MS. This approach should not be taken to imply that we believe that an originally very literal Targum was later revised and expanded. The actual processes which led to the production of the Targumim are demonstrably more complex than this, and it is well known that the Palestinian Targum contains much early tradition in its 'additional' material.[7]

THE PESHITTA

The only place mentioned in the itineraries which the Peshitta identifies in terms of later geographical names is Kadesh. In

Num. 20: 1, 22 Kadesh is represented by רקם.[8] רקם is evidently the Semitic name for Petra,[9] and this name stands in place of 'Kadesh' in all the Targumim. We have already noted that for Josephus Mount Hor was near Petra, and now it appears that there was an authoritative tradition which actually identified Petra as the site of Kadesh. Josephus seems to know nothing of this tradition, at least he makes no mention of it in a passage where he could easily have done so (AJ 4.82). It is very difficult to find early datable references to Petra as the site of Kadesh, which is surprising in view of the uniformity of the Targumim at this point. In his *Onomasticon* (cf. below, p. 33) Eusebius speaks of Kadesh as being not exactly *at* Petra but the name of the desert bordering Petra. It is possible then that the actual identification of Kadesh with Petra was a later development still.

Yet it may be questioned whether an account of the traditions that came to be associated with Petra which is based solely on the datable evidence is entirely adequate. In particular it is unclear why a very tenacious link should have been forged between Mount Hor of the Bible and the area around Petra, unless there was already a strong reason for looking for Mount Hor in that region. By contrast, there are a number of reasons which could have given rise to the identification of Kadesh with Petra. I have suggested elsewhere that the confusion of two places both known by the name Reqem may have been responsible.[10] It is also possible that the reference to Kadesh as a 'city' in Num. 20: 13 led to its being identified with the only settlement in the far south which was of major importance. Petra may have seemed an appropriate site for one or more of the events associated with Kadesh in the Old Testament: the gift of water from the rock (Num. 20: 11), a prolonged stay by a large company of people (Dt. 1: 46), or even, as P. S. Alexander has suggested, the death of Korah and his companions.[11] Another possibility is that Petra seemed to be in the right position, about half-way between Aila on the Gulf of Akaba and Phaeno(n) (modern Khirbet Feinan), for a place which in the most detailed wilderness itinerary came between

Ezion-Geber and Punon, which were identified with these sites. There are so many reasons for putting Kadesh at Petra and none at all that we know for putting Mount Hor there that it seems that Kadesh *must* have been located there first, and Mount Hor only subsequently!

In two other passages the Peshitta gives a different rendering of the itineraries from what MT would lead one to expect (Num. 21: 11–18; 33: 44–5, 47–8), but these variants do not permit any geographical conclusions to be drawn.

THE TARGUM OF ONKELOS

In addition to rendering 'Kadesh' by רקם Onkelos gives a contemporary equivalent for the toponym 'Shur', which occurs in the expression 'the Wilderness of Shur' in Ex. 15: 22. This expression is rendered by חגרא, מדברא דחגרא being the term used by Onkelos and Jonathan for 'Shur' in all its occurrences in the Pentateuch and the Former Prophets. חגרא is a term which occurs in other Rabbinic texts and apparently referred to the border area south of the cultivable land of Palestine.[12] Thus the area into which Israel passed after crossing 'the sea' was defined by reference to Palestine itself, and this may have suggested to some readers of the Targum that the people had approached the promised land early in their wilderness journey. But with as vague a term as מדברא דחגרא seems to be it is impossible to argue that this is what the rendering was intended to convey.

Onkelos too has a number of variants in the representations of the names in the itineraries which are of no geographical significance, several of them shared with the Peshitta, which confirms the appropriateness of treating the Peshitta along with the Targumim.[13]

TARGUM YERUSHALMI II

The different forms of the Palestinian Targum exhibit considerably more attempts to localise the places named in the itineraries. Several of the interpretations are found in all the preserved texts, but others only in Pseudo-Jonathan or in the Fragmentary Targum and the Neofiti MS., which are the main representatives of the Targum Yerushalmi II tradition. We deal first with those which appear either in all 'Palestinian' texts or in those representing Targum Yerushalmi II.

It may first be noted that the rendering of 'Kadesh' by רקם is normal in these texts, just as in the Peshitta and Onkelos. 'Shur' in Ex. 15: 22 is not however represented by חגרא, as in Onkelos, but by חלוצא, the name of a town in the Negeb founded by the Nabataeans which had considerable importance as a centre of religious life and local administration in the later Roman Empire and even under the Arabs. It is located some 15 miles (24 km) south-west of Beersheba: the modern Arab name of al-Khalaṣa together with entries on ancient maps leaves no doubt about its identification.[14] Thus again, as was the case in Onkelos, 'Shur' is located by reference to a term drawn from the south of Palestine. It is readily understandable how the name חלוצא was introduced into the Targum, if this happened after 358 AD, when Halutsa became the 'capital' of Palaestina Tertia. But Halutsa had a long history before this, and it is quite possible that the 'Palestinian' identification of the Wilderness of Shur originated at an earlier date.

Two places which are not given any interpretation in the Peshitta and Onkelos – they are merely transcribed – are identified in all texts of the Palestinian Targum. The first is Rameses, which is equated with Pelusium on the Mediterranean coast at the eastern extremity of the Nile delta.[15] This corresponds to one view about the Israelites' settlement in Egypt which is attested in Josephus (see p. 13 above on the *Contra Apionem*), an interesting example of the common background which can sometimes be traced between Jewish texts written in Greek and those written in Hebrew or Aramaic. In this case the parallel shows that the Palestinian Targum texts preserve here a tradition which can be traced back at least to the middle of the first century AD.

The other place to receive an identification in these texts is Ezion-Geber, which is rendered as כרך תרנגולא, 'the city (or fortress) of the cock'. The second part of the name is undoubtedly based on the fact that in Aramaic and post-

Biblical Hebrew גבר can mean 'cock', and is an example of the translation of the meaning of a name, which is a practice employed elsewhere in the Palestinian Targum texts.[16] It is not so clear why כרך was thought to be an acceptable equivalent for עצין, which is an obscure name, perhaps referring to a kind of vegetation prevalent at the place.[17] It may be relevant that the location of Ezion-Geber was fixed already in Josephus' time as 'not far from the city of Aelana [= Aila]' (AJ 8.163), and that in Eusebius' *Onomasticon*[18] it was specifically identified with a place near Aila called Aisia or Asia. Perhaps the 'city' referred to in the Targumic rendering was either this (otherwise practically unknown) place Aisia/Asia or, better, the 'city' (Josephus' term) of Aila itself. In the absence of any obvious way of explaining כרך as a translation of עצין, it is natural to look for a reference to a particular place in it, the more so when we bear in mind that Ezion-Geber was a place associated with a definite locality in Jewish tradition from at least the first century AD onwards.

There is one interpretation of a name in the itineraries which is of interest more because it is only found in Targum Yerushalmi II texts than for any light which it might shed on the way in which Jews conceived of the route of the Israelites through the wilderness. This is the rendering of 'Pi-hahiroth' by פונדקי חירתא, 'inns of licentiousness', apparently 'brothels'. While the meaning given for the second part of the name is clearly based on the assumption that it is the post-Biblical Hebrew word חרות, 'freedom', the use of a word meaning 'inns' for פי (which in Hebrew means 'mouth of' – cf. the translations of this name in other Targum texts) is difficult to explain. It is a possibility worth considering that this interpretation is based on knowledge that in Egyptian *Per-* (sometimes abbreviated to *Pi-*: cf. the customary analysis of פתם in Ex. 1: 11 as equivalent to *Pi-Atum*) meant 'house (of)'. This knowledge would presumably have been available in an Egyptian Jewish community, where the interpretation of the name may have originated. No clue to the place associated with the crossing of the sea can be gleaned from this rendering –

indeed it is most probable that it was not intended to refer to a particular place at all. But the fact that in it Targum Yerushalmi II has a peculiar reading, while there are several interpretations in Pseudo-Jonathan which do not appear in it (see below), is evidence that the relationship between these two forms of the Palestinian Targum tradition is not a simple and direct one, however much that may be suggested by the interpretations which they share.

TARGUM YERUSHALMI I (PSEUDO-JONATHAN)

In its identifications of Kadesh, the Wilderness of Shur, Rameses and Ezion-Geber Pseudo-Jonathan agrees with Targum Yerushalmi II. But it also includes quite precise interpretative matter of a geographical kind at five points where the texts of the latter are content with either simple transcription of the names or with non-geographical interpretations. Thus in the case of Pi-hahiroth, Pseudo-Jonathan has a much more involved explanation which shows no acquaintance with the interpretation of פי by פונדקי, to which he then tacks on the statement that the place meant is Tanis. This was a well-known place in the Nile delta which gave its name to one of the branches of the Nile, and it is generally identified with the modern site of San el-Hajar.[19] This would imply that the crossing of the sea took place somewhere in the north of the isthmus of Suez, after the Israelites had made a westerly journey of about 35 miles (56 km) from Pelusium, which Pseudo-Jonathan too regarded as the site of Rameses. This is a curious route and a curious location for 'the sea' in view of the tradition which placed the latter at the Gulf of Suez. If those responsible for the identification of Pi-hahiroth and Tanis had any concern for geography, one would expect there to be a strong reason for their having adopted it. Such a reason can be found in Ps. 78: 12–13, which could be taken to mean that the 'dividing of the sea' was one of the marvels performed in 'the field(s) of Zoan', the older name for Tanis.

The age of this tradition is difficult to determine. Tanis

appears in all the Palestinian Targum texts at Ex. 1: 11 as the
equivalent to Pithom; this interpretation could have been due
to a different (and probably correct) reading of Ps. 78: 12–13,
which saw these verses as referring to different stages of the
Exodus story, the first (which mentions Zoan/Tanis) applying
to the plagues and the second to the deliverance itself. Now
according to the Mekhilta, a basically Tannaitic midrash on
parts of Exodus, 'Pi-hahiroth' was only a new name for the
place traditionally called 'Pithom'.[20] It is possible that this view
arose simply because the two names were rather similar. But it
is also possible that it presupposes the identification of both
Pithom and Pi-hahiroth with one place, Tanis. In that case
there would be a reason for thinking that the tradition used by
Pseudo-Jonathan alone of the Targumim originated as early as
the Tannaitic period.

Pseudo-Jonathan also offers an interpretation of a less well-
known name in the itineraries, that of Alush (Num. 33: 13–
14). This is rendered כרך תקיף, 'a mighty city [or fortress]'.
This is not a precise identification, but it may well be an
allusion to a Rabbinic tradition that Alush was another name
for Halutsa in the south of Palestine. This covert equation of
Alush with a well-known city may well also be presupposed by
the reference in B. Yoma 10a to the building of a place called
Alush by one of 'the sons of Anak'.[21] There can be little doubt
that this is associated in some way with Pseudo-Jonathan's
rendering of the name Alush in the itinerary, and since the
Old Testament has 'the sons of Anak' living at Hebron it is
much more likely that one of them was thought to have built
the important city of Halutsa in the Negeb than that another
Alush in Mesopotamia is meant.[22] Since the Wilderness of
Shur had already been equated in Pseudo-Jonathan with 'the
Wilderness of Halutsa', it would have been a reasonable enough
step to see Halutsa itself as the site of a following station. There
is no positive evidence for regarding this identification as
Tannaitic in origin, and perhaps it is most likely to have gained
acceptance when Halutsa had attained the zenith of its importance in the fourth century AD.

The next interpretation to be considered does not involve the introduction of a more up-to-date place-name either. In Num. 10: 33, one of the verses which describe Israel's departure from Mount Sinai, Pseudo-Jonathan has an extensive elaboration of MT, and has the ark cover 'the journey of three days' in a single day. What is most interesting is that the text mentions the figure of 36 Roman miles (53 km) as the distance that was covered. What can be the basis for this? It can hardly be that this distance was thought to be either that which might be covered in one day or in three, as the normal figure for a day's journey in the ancient world was about 20 miles (32 km).[23] The same figure of 36 Roman miles appears in an exposition of the verse attributed to R. Simeon b. Yochai (second century AD),[24] which shows that it is a relatively early element of tradition, but the context does not indicate the basis for this calculation. In these circumstances some speculation about what could have produced the figure is justifiable.

According to the other verse that reports the Israelites' departure from Mount Sinai, Num. 10: 12, their first major camping-place after the Wilderness of Sinai was the Wilderness of Paran. It is fully to be expected that the Rabbinic study of Num. 10 would have noted the parallelism between verses 12 and 33, and even have allowed the contents of the one to have influenced the interpretation of the other. In all probability the Wilderness of Sinai and the Wilderness of Paran were two widely separated areas. But at some point before the fourth century AD the tradition arose that they were quite close together, both located in the south of the Sinai Peninsula. This is already the view of Eusebius in his *Onomasticon* (for fuller discussion see below, pp. 31–2), and it was the view of a succession of Christians who visited or wrote about the area. Whatever may be the origin of the view that Mount Sinai was located there, it is not difficult to see why the Wilderness of Paran was thought to be in the south (rather than the north) of the Sinai peninsula. There was, not far from the tip of the peninsula, a town called in Greek Φαράν (Ptolemy, *Geography* 6.17.1) – the name is probably preserved in the modern Arabic name of Wadi Feiran, a large valley which leads up from the Gulf of Suez to the southern mountain massif.[25] Φαράν is the Greek form which, by the normal procedure adopted in LXX for the transcription of proper names, was used in Greek for 'Paran'. Once this had been done, it was natural for a reader of LXX to suppose that the town in southern Sinai was referred to when Φαράν was mentioned. But it need not have been in the Greek-speaking world that this equation was first made. A speaker of a Semitic language would have no way of distinguishing between the name of the town in southern Sinai and that of the wilderness mentioned in the book of Numbers.

The Christian pilgrim Etheria, who visited holy places in the Sinai peninsula and elsewhere towards the end of the fourth century AD, gave the distance between Mount Sinai and 'Faran' as 35 miles (51 km) (*Peregrinatio* 6.1). In view of the location of Faran (the town), which is generally agreed to have been the tell which rises at the northern end of the oasis of Wadi Feiran, the distance given and the description of 'Mount Sinai' and its surroundings in the *Peregrinatio* (chs. 1–5), 'her' Mount Sinai must have been Jebel Musa or, less likely, a neighbouring peak.[26] This identification of Mount Sinai is often dubbed the 'Christian' view.[27] But if it and the location of the Wilderness of Paran near Faran were already current in the second century AD among Jews, then the enigmatic figure of '36 miles' (53 km) in R. Simeon b. Yochai's interpretation of Num. 10:33 would receive a simple explanation as a cryptic reference to the distance between what were thought to be the sites of the Wilderness of Sinai and the Wilderness of Paran. Until some more probable account of the figure in this Jewish interpretation is forthcoming, it must be regarded as likely that the identifications of Mount Sinai and the Wilderness of Paran, which appear in the works of Eusebius and Etheria, have a Jewish origin in the Tannaitic period.[28]

Two interpretations of names towards the end of the itineraries are also found in Pseudo-Jonathan and not in the other Targum texts. In one case, 'the Wilderness of Zin', the interpretation is found only in the Targum's rendering of

Num. 33 (verse 36), and not in other passages where the Israelites' stay there is mentioned. The equivalent given is 'the wilderness of the thorn-palms (צִינִי) of the mountain of iron'. Clearly there is a play here on the similarity of the name 'Zin' and the word for 'thorn-palms'. 'The thorn-palms of the mountain of iron' were famous, and gave rise to a halakhic ruling (cf. Sukk. 3.1): 'The thorn-palms of the mountain of iron are valid' (sc. for the *lulab*). The location of 'the mountain of iron' is implied by Josephus (*Bellum Judaicum* 4.454) to have been east of the Dead Sea.[29] To associate it, as Pseudo-Jonathan does in Num. 33: 36, with Kadesh = Petra is therefore rather unnatural, and probably explains why this identification was not generally adopted in the text. The source from which it was introduced into Num. 33: 36 (possibly by a copyist rather than in the context of the thoroughgoing interpretation of the text which was responsible for the consistent adoption of some other equivalences) was probably the account of the southern border of the land of Canaan at the beginning of the following chapter, where Pseudo-Jonathan represents 'Zin' (Num. 34: 4) by the same phrase. There its use is not unnatural, as it is the next boundary-point to Kadesh, and not identical with it. Although the name used in the interpretation is one attested in the first century AD (Josephus), it is not certain that this tradition is as old as that – other evidence of the identification is lacking.[30]

The final identification in Pseudo-Jonathan to be considered is that of Mount Hor with טוורוס אומנוס, 'Taurus Amanus', which is found in all the itinerary-passages which mention it.[31] Mount Amanus was a southerly extension of the Taurus range (Strabo, *Geography* 11.12.2, 12.2.2), which reached the mouth of the Orontes river in Syria.[32] The combination of names in the Targum is not found in Strabo, but it clearly means 'that part of the Taurus which is known as the Amanus'. What is surprising is that any place named in the wilderness itineraries should have been thought to be so far to the north of Palestine. But the explanation lies close at hand. There was another Mount Hor on the northern boundary of the land of Canaan (Num. 34: 7–8), which was probably in actual fact near to Byblos.[33] But in all the Palestinian Targum texts it was equated with the Amanus 150 miles (240 km) further north. The reason for this will have been the desire to harmonise the different accounts of the boundaries of the land given to Israel, one of which (Gen. 15: 18) spoke of it as extending to the Euphrates. The view that the Amanus was the northern limit of 'the land', at least according to one definition of it, seems to be presupposed in a passage in the Mishna (Sheb. 6.1), and so its identification with the northern Mount Hor was probably already current at that time, and represents another Tannaitic element in the Palestinian Targum tradition. But the same cannot be said for the equation of the southern Mount Hor with it, which is clearly due simply to a failure to realise or take note of the fact that there were two distinct mountains of the same name. In fact Pseudo-Jonathan's identification of the southern Mount Hor runs clean counter to the tradition in Josephus (and Eusebius) that it was close to Petra.

In addition to the items of geographical interest that have been discussed in detail, the Palestinian Targum texts contain much other interpretative material related to the itineraries. Some of this corresponds to what is found in Onkelos, but there is also further material, especially in Num. 21: 16–20 (where the 'itinerary of the well' motif is developed) and at Dt. 10: 6–7 (where Pseudo-Jonathan has what seems to be a rather late treatment of a problem of harmonisation which was already discussed in the Tannaitic period).[34]

THE MIDRASHIM

We have examined the relevant passages of the Mekhilta, Sifre on Numbers and Midrash Rabbah on Exodus and Numbers, to see whether they include geographical interpretations of the itineraries. Of these Sifre, apart from the exegesis of R. Simeon b. Yochai already discussed in connection with Pseudo-Jonathan, and Midrash Rabbah contain nothing of relevance to our subject. The Mekhilta does, however, have three further passages of some interest, in addition to those already cited in connection with various Targumic interpretations.

In the comment on Ex. 12: 37 the distance from Rameses to Succoth is said to be 120 Persian miles (i.e. parasangs).[35] As the following sentence makes clear, this resulted from the identification of Succoth in the itinerary with the place visited by Jacob (Gen. 33: 17), which was in Transjordan. This is the same kind of mistake as led to Pseudo-Jonathan's location of Mount Hor (the southern one) at the Amanus.[36] The difficulty of so great a distance being covered in a single day is answered by a reference to Ex. 19: 4: 'You have seen... how I bore you on eagles' wings and brought you to myself.' Yet alongside these fanciful discussions of the text the Mekhilta includes the much more sober opinion of 'other sages' who held, in the light of the itinerary in Num. 33, that Succoth was just a place like Etham, which followed it in the list. This comment deserves comparison with those attributed to R. Eliezer in connection with the etymologising interpretations of the names Rephidim and Shittim.[37]

A similar contrast emerges in the interpretations of Ex. 14: 2 attributed to R. Eliezer and R. Joshua.[38] The question at issue is the nature of החירת. R. Eliezer gave an imaginative description of them (which reappears in the Targum of Pseudo-Jonathan on this verse), but R. Joshua treated the term simply as a name: 'The חירת were on one side and Migdol on the other, with the sea in front of them and Egypt/the Egyptians behind them.' It is interesting that this description does not correspond exactly to the account of the encampment by the sea in MT. Perhaps the relationship between the places named had been adjusted to fit in with identifications of them that were accepted at that time. But if this was the case, it is of no help to us in our attempt to trace the history of the location of places mentioned in the wilderness itineraries, as even the advocates of a straightforward interpretation of the names give no indication of where they thought that the places were.

The third comment of a geographical nature in the Mekhilta which remains to be noted is the interpretation[39] of נגד in Ex. 19: 2 as meaning 'east of', so that the camp of Israel is placed to the east of Mount Sinai. Such a meaning for נגד is hard to parallel in the Old Testament, where it can usually be translated 'opposite', and it seems to have been arrived at on the analogy of other Hebrew words for 'opposite' or 'before' which were used to mean 'east of', such as קדם(מ) and על פני. It is tempting to suggest that this unusual rendering of נגד was adopted because there was a space on the east of the mountain identified as Mount Sinai, where the camp of Israel was supposed to have been – Wadi ed-Deir below Jebel Musa, where St Catherine's Monastery now stands? But even if this is so, the Mekhilta gives no further indication of the identity of the mountain involved.

RASHI

As in other matters, so in his treatment of the itineraries Rashi was frequently content to restate conclusions already stated in the Targumim and Midrashim or in the Talmud. These include some points of geographical interest, such as the dimensions of the Israelite encampment by the Jordan (deduced from its limits), but he seems more interested in other kinds of problems posed by these texts. There are two comments of his which may be original that are of some relevance to our theme. In his comment on Ex. 13: 18 he proposed the now widely accepted interpretation of the meaning of ים סוף: 'סוף means a swamp in which reeds grow, as (Ex. 2: 3): "She put it into the reeds".' In fact there is a partial precedent for this in a passage of Jerome, but he seems not to have thought it relevant to all occurrences of ים סוף, but only to one which caused him some difficulty.[40] Rashi also endeavoured to make geographical sense of the difficult verse Num. 21: 13. He did this by suggesting that there was a strip of Amorite land which extended through what was basically Moabite territory to the Arnon. But because he must harmonise this verse with the statement of Jud. 11: 18 that Israel did not cross the territory of Moab, he is led into assuming that they made a very mysterious detour around Moab and then back into the middle of it on Amorite land.

If these two examples can be taken as a fair illustration of Rashi's contribution to Biblical geography, they show him as, on the one hand, a figure with the philological equipment that is essential for understanding the Biblical texts, but, on the other, one who deploys his ingenuity to harmonise different texts and explain difficult ones, even where the result is historically or geographically improbable. It is emphatically the approach of the grammarian, in both its strength and its weakness, rather than that of the explorer.

The examination of the treatment of the itineraries in the Targumim made clear that there is a side to Jewish interpretation of the Bible which is often neglected. The Jewish exegetes were not only interested in the itineraries as texts for edifying teaching and sources for exegetical controversy. In the Targumim there emerges, along with these well-known characteristics, a genuine geographical interest, parallel in nature if not in extent to that found in some branches of traditional Christian interpretation of the Bible. The common picture of Jewish exegesis is perhaps distorted a little by being based too much on the Midrashim, where, as we have seen, geographical interest is much less apparent. True, it has been possible in some cases to find echoes of the Targumic identifications of places in the Midrashim. But they are few in number, and significantly they usually involve the discussion of some problem arising out of a geographical interpretation which is of theological or practical interest. This kind of literature does not advance but presupposes the kind of topographical 'knowledge' which we have encountered in the Targumim. In this respect Rashi must for the most part be classified with the Midrashim.

CHAPTER 4

CHRISTIAN INTERPRETATIONS

In surviving Christian literature of the first three centuries AD there is surprisingly little evidence of any acquaintance with a geographical interpretation of the wilderness itineraries, despite the fact that by this time, as we have seen, a number of identifications were current in Jewish circles. The 'sea' of Exodus was of course equated with the Red Sea (cf. Acts 7: 36; Heb. 11: 29), following the rendering given in LXX. Other than this only indications of the location of Mount Sinai (and vague ones at that) are found. Paul located it in 'Arabia' (Gal. 4: 25), but in view of the wide area covered by this term, which included the Sinai peninsula as well as Arabia proper,[1] we at any rate cannot be sure where Paul thought it was, even if he himself was acquainted with a specific local tradition.[2] A third-century anti-Jewish tract ascribed to Cyprian put Mount Sinai in Palestine,[3] which was at that time a shortened form of the name of the Roman province of Syria Palaestina, whose southern border was in the northern Negeb.[4] The inclusion of the Sinai peninsula in 'Palestine' was only possible after the reorganisation of the area at about 300 AD which added most of what had hitherto been Arabia Petraea to Palestine,[5] and seems to be first attested in the sixth century.[6] This could be taken to mean that Pseudo-Cyprian knew a tradition that Mount Sinai was in the hill country in the south of Palestine proper. But he shows no interest in geographical detail and he may have had only an imprecise idea of the geography of the area.[7]

The absence of more detailed traditions about the route of the Israelites can probably be attributed to the fact that pilgrimages to the Holy Land only became common among Christians in the fourth century.[8] The earliest text to give the kind of information in which we are interested is the *Onomasticon* of Eusebius, which he compiled before 330. Jerome's *Liber de situ et nominibus locorum hebraicorum* is a translation of the *Onomasticon*, with some revisions, made about 390.[9] Despite the differences between the Greek and Latin texts, they can most conveniently be treated together here.

EUSEBIUS AND JEROME

Even Eusebius and Jerome give geographical information about fewer than half the places mentioned in the itineraries. Many places are merely described as σταθμὸς τῶν υἱῶν ᾽Ισραὴλ ἐπὶ τῆς ἐρήμου or something similar,[10] and some are passed over completely, at least by Eusebius.[11] What is particularly striking is that there is no interest in the place of the crossing of the Red Sea or the location of the Egyptian places which had already by this time been identified in Jewish tradition. For the first part of the route all that these authors offer is the traditional equation of Yam Suf with ἡ ἐρυθρὰ θάλασσα or *mare rubrum*.[12] This suggests that their works were compiled from traditions available in Palestine itself, where both of them spent most of their scholarly life.

The identifications which they record are grouped for the most part around three areas: the neighbourhood of Faran in the south of the Sinai peninsula, the area east of Wadi Arabah (especially around Petra) and the region east and north-east of the Dead Sea.[13] This is no doubt due partly to the fact that in two, and probably all three, of these areas Jewish tradition had long located places mentioned in the itineraries. But in number the traditions have so increased that it is probably correct to envisage these areas as being more and more frequently visited by those anxious to find traces of sacred history in them. Nor should the contribution made by the local communities of places like Faran, Petra and Livias be underestimated.

The place which Faran in southern Sinai came to occupy in the accepted localisation of the Israelites' journeys has already been touched on above (p. 23). Eusebius has the following entry for Φαράν:

πόλις ἐστὶν ὑπὲρ τὴν Ἀραβίαν, παρακειμένη τοῖς ἐπὶ τῆς ἐρήμου Σαρακηνοῖς, δι' ἧς ὥδευσαν οἱ υἱοὶ Ἰσραήλ, ἀπάραντες ἀπὸ Σινᾶ. κεῖται δὲ καὶ ἐπέκεινα τῆς Ἀραβίας ἐπὶ νότον.[14]

The reference to Φαράν as a πόλις 'beyond' or 'to the south of' Arabia fits exactly the location for Faran indicated by Ptolemy, and there can be little doubt, in the absence of other suitable sites in the area, that its remains are to be found at Tell el-Mekharet (or Makhrad) at the north end of the oasis in Wadi Feiran. The site has not been excavated yet, but it is clear from visible remains of buildings and surface pottery that it was important in both the Nabataean and Byzantine periods.[15]

The entry in the *Onomasticon* continues:

ἀπέχει δὲ Ἀϊλὰ πρὸς ἀνατολὰς ὁδὸν τριῶν ἡμερῶν.[16]

This clearly can, and does, mean that Aila was (broadly speaking) east of Faran. But Jerome, apparently ignorant of the geographical facts at this time at least, translated it:

et distat ab Aila contra orientem itinere trium dierum.[17]

Since Aila was at the head of the Gulf of Akaba, this would put Faran in modern Arabia!

According to Eusebius (and Jerome) Israel passed through Faran – or the desert beside it – after leaving Mount Sinai. This will mean that they identified it as the place referred to in the Biblical toponym 'the Wilderness of Paran'.[18] Another entry in the *Onomasticon* shows that both Rephidim and Mount Horeb were also considered to be close to Faran.

Ῥαφιδίμ. τόπος τῆς ἐρήμου παρὰ τὸ Χωρὴβ ὄρος, ἐν ᾧ ἐκ τῆς πέτρας τῆς ἐν τῷ ὄρει Χωρὴβ ἐρρύησαν τὰ ὕδατα. καὶ ἐκλήθη ὁ τόπος πειρασμός. ἔνθα καὶ πολεμεῖ Ἰησοῦς τὸν Ἀμαλὴκ ἐγγὺς Φαράν.[19]

The entry for 'Horeb' is:

ὄρος τοῦ θεοῦ ἐν χώρᾳ Μαδιάμ. παράκειται τῷ ὄρει Σινᾶ ὑπὲρ τὴν Ἀραβίαν ἐπὶ τῆς ἐρήμου.[20]

This is compatible with a location in southern Sinai, which is required by the 'Rephidim' entry, when it is realised that the first part of it, including the words ἐν χώρᾳ Μαδιάμ, is not an attempt to localise Horeb in terms of a contemporary place-name, but a reference to Biblical nomenclature such as often appears in the *Onomasticon* (cf. Ex. 2 : 15). The same entry shows that Eusebius regarded Horeb and Sinai as distinct but adjacent mountains – there is in fact no entry for Mount Sinai itself in the *Onomasticon*. Jerome holds a slightly different view, which he may simply have deduced from the text of the Bible, that they are different names for the same place.[21]

From what Eusebius and Jerome say it is not possible to tell which of the mountains in the south of the Sinai peninsula was regarded as Mount Horeb. Undoubtedly Jebel Serbal, which some scholars have thought to be meant,[22] is nearer to Faran than Jebel Musa is, but in such a desolate area the more distant mountain could easily have been spoken of as 'near' to Faran, as it was nearer to there than to any other place of note. The only way in which a decision can be made is by reasoning back from clearer passages of a later date. To anticipate the detailed discussion of passages of Ammonius, Etheria and Cosmas Indicopleustes below, we have reached the conclusion that the only unambiguous evidence (Etheria, *Peregrinatio* 6.1; and, from the period after Justinian had his monastery built, Antoninus, *Itinerarium* 37) points to the equation of Mount Sinai with Jebel Musa, but that Mount Horeb was variously identified and by some was held to be very close to Faran, possibly Jebel Serbal. The evidence for this latter tradition is however only extant for the sixth century (Cosmas), so that it must remain doubtful whether Eusebius knew it.[23] 55114

At the centre of the second group of identifications are two which are paralleled in Jewish tradition. Both Mount Hor[24] and Kadesh[25] (which is regarded as the name of a wilderness rather than a place) are said to be close to Petra. In the entries for these places Eusebius records that Miriam's tomb and the rock from which Moses caused water to flow were pointed out to visitors to the area. In addition the place where Aaron died is said (in the entry for 'Beeroth Bene-jaakan')[26] to have been 10 σημεῖα (Eusebius' usual word for 'mile(stone)s') from Petra. This suggests that some mountain other than Jebel Harun, which has more recently been regarded as the site of Aaron's

33

death, must be meant, as it is only about 5 miles (8 km) from the site of Petra.

Other places to be associated with Petra are Punon/Pinon[27] and Iyye-haabarim.[28] The former is said to be between Petra and Zoar and is identified with a contemporary mining site, Φαινών, to which there are a number of other references in ancient literature.[29] Clearly in this case the similarity of the names has led to the equation, and it is generally agreed that it is a correct one. The inclusion of Iyye-haabarim is more surprising, as according to Num. 33: 44 it was 'in the territory (or on the border) of Moab' and therefore well to the north of Petra. It is in fact said by Eusebius to be the same as a 'city' called Gaia adjacent to Petra. The name still survives in the area as el-Ji. The reason for the identification of Iyye-haabarim with it is that the LXX rendering for that name, which Eusebius reproduces in his entry, is Γαί, with ע being transcribed as γ, a not infrequent equivalence which presumably reflects a 'strong' pronunciation of ע in some words. This identification was presumably made by someone who spoke Greek, as in a Semitic language there would be no reason to identify places whose names begin with א and ע.

Eusebius actually has another entry for Iyye-haabarim in the form Αἰή, which is the transcription given in the (hexaplaric) cursive MS. of LXX x at Num. 21: 11.[30] Here he gives a more reasonable location for the place, to the east of Moab, obviously being guided here by the data of the Biblical text. This is not the only place where Eusebius has two entries for the same place because of different LXX/hexaplaric transcriptions, but it is surprising to find different identifications suggested.

Another place thought to be in the region of Wadi Arabah, but not explicitly connected with Petra, was Ezion-Geber, which was identified by Eusebius with a place called Aisia or Asia,[31] close to Aila on the Gulf of Akaba. In view of the passages which conjoin Ezion-Geber and Elath, the name of which lived on in 'Aila', in the Old Testament (cf. Dt. 2: 8; 1 Ki. 9: 26), it is not difficult to see how such an identification might arise, especially as the names Ἀσιών, one transcription of עצי, and 'Aσία/Aἰσία are so similar. It may even be that this fourth-century name was in fact a Hellenised version of עצי. Unfortunately it is impossible at present to locate Asia/ Aisia exactly, as no similar name has been reported near Akaba[32] and there are no other literary references to it.

The third group of identifications may be subdivided into those which are connected with 'the Arnon' and those which refer to the site of Israel's final encampment before they crossed the Jordan. For Eusebius 'the Arnon' was not the name of a valley, as it has generally been understood in modern times, but the name of a rugged area to the north of Rabbath Moab, or to give it its Greek name, Areopolis. In this he was following the nomenclature of his day:

δείκνυται δὲ εἰς ἔτι νῦν τόπος φαραγγώδης σφόδρα χαλεπὸς ὁ 'Αρνωνᾶ ὀνομαζόμενος, παρατείνων ἐπὶ τὰ βόρεια τῆς 'Αρεοπόλεως, ἐν ᾧ καὶ φρούρια πανταχόθεν φυλάττει στρατιωτικὰ διὰ τὸ φοβερὸν τοῦ τόπου.[33]

The reference to numerous garrisons shows that an area of some extent is envisaged.[34] The four stations mentioned in Num. 21: 19–20 are all associated by Eusebius with 'the Arnon' so understood. Mattanah is equated with a place Maschana, 12 miles (19 km) east of Madeba, and said to be ἐπὶ τοῦ 'Αρνωνᾶ.[35] For the other places, Nahaliel, Bamoth and Ianna, no precise location is offered: they are said to be πλησίον, ἐν, or παρά 'the Arnon'.[36] The reason for Eusebius' association of these places with 'the Arnon' is not completely clear, although it was facilitated by his conception of the latter as a region. The most likely explanation is that Eusebius (or his source) deduced from the context that the Israelites were at this stage still in the region which they had entered according to Num. 21: 13, the border region between Moab and the Amorites, called 'the Arnon'; for in verse 22 they still have to ask Sihon's permission to pass through his territory.

The *Onomasticon* has identifications for most of the places mentioned in connection with the final encampment in Transjordan. Of the two places which are said in Num. 33: 49 to have been the limits of the camp, Beth-jeshimoth is located in the territory of Isemuth, 10 miles (16 km) south of Jericho by the Dead Sea – Jerome says that there was a village of that name in his own day, and the name has been thought to be preserved as es-Suweimeh.[37] Abel-shittim is not precisely located in its own entry, being stated simply to be κατὰ δυσμὰς Μωάβ, the common LXX rendering for 'in the plains of Moab', ערבות being mistakenly thought to be connected with מערב = 'west'.[38] This information has simply been extracted from LXX of Num. 33: 49. No doubt is left, however, about the location of Abel-shittim, because 'the plains of Moab' is one of a number of places which is quite precisely located by reference to a well-known road (see below). Thus far Eusebius presents information about places also identified in Rabbinic tradition, and although we cannot be sure that the same identifications were envisaged this is quite possible, as the places referred to by Eusebius were about 'three Persian miles' (about 10 English miles, or 16 km) apart (see above, p. 15).

The road with reference to which the other places in this area were pinpointed is the Roman road from Livias (Tell er-Rame) to Esebus (Tell Hesban/Heshbon).[39] 'The plains of Moab' are said to be 'beside Mount Peor',[40] which is 'alongside the road going up from Livias to Esebus'.[41] The road ascends by the ridge south of Wadi Hesban, and Peor is presumably identified with this high ground. The 'plains of Moab' will then have been taken to be either in Wadi Hesban itself or further to the west at the point where it enters the Jordan valley. Two related places are located by Eusebius with reference to the sixth milestone on the Livias–Esebus road. Beth-peor (cf. Dt. 3: 29; 4: 46) is said to be 'six milestones' above Livias;[42] and Mount Nebo was pointed out ἀπὸ ἕκτου σημείου Ἐσβοῦς εἰς δυσμάς (which may mean the sixth milestone *from* Esebus, though given the distance between the two places it would also be the sixth milestone from Livias) – across the intervening valley, if we may assume that the site which later became traditional is meant.[43] Shittim, which in the *Onomasticon* is just said to be 'beside Mount Peor',[44] is also located here by Jerome in his comment on the expression 'the fountain of Shittim' in Joel 4: 18:

locus iuxta Liviadem trans mare mortuum sexto ab ea [sc. Livias] distans milliario.[45]

The sixth milestone from Livias lay at the very end of the summit of the ridge and the ruins of a Roman fortress have recently been found nearby.[46]

AMMONIUS

Two of the accounts which purport to describe visits to Mount Sinai in the century after Eusebius contain information which has sometimes been thought to permit a definite conclusion that Mount Sinai was then considered to be very close to Faran, in fact to be Jebel Serbal. Of these the *Narrationes* of Nilus would be of little value for our purpose even if they were authentic fourth-century compositions, because they only show that the monastic community of Mount Sinai lived in the general vicinity of Faran.[47] Since Faran was the only settlement of any significance in southern Sinai apart from Raithu (on which see below), this need not be an at all precise indication of their position.[48]

The other document is the *Treatise on the murder of the Holy Fathers of Mount Sinai and Raithu* attributed to a monk called Ammonius, who writes as though he had been present at Mount Sinai when the community there was attacked by marauding Saracens.[49] It has been claimed that this too is historically worthless.[50] But although the speech ascribed to Paul, the leader of the Raithu community, looks as though it has been written up in the Thucydidean manner, in general the arguments against the work's genuineness are not as persuasive as those levelled against the *Narrationes* of Nilus.

According to Ammonius Mount Sinai was eighteen days' journey from Jerusalem and two days' journey from Raithu, which is probably to be identified with et-Tur on the west coast of the peninsula a little to the south of the latitude of Jebel Musa.[51] M. Harel gives the distance from et-Tur to Faran as 72 km (= 45 miles) and from et-Tur to St Catherine's Monastery, below Jebel Musa, as 130 km (= 81 miles), and argues that Ammonius must have known a Mount Sinai in the immediate vicinity of Faran.[52] Yet if that were the case, it is curious that the inhabitants of Faran intervened when Raithu was attacked and not when the Mount Sinai community was in danger. Moreover, Harel assumes that the route from et-Tur to St Catherine's went via Faran, when there are more direct routes through the mountains via Wadi Hibran or Wadi Islah which could be covered in two days. There is therefore no need to think that Ammonius knew a Mount Sinai in the immediate vicinity of Faran, and the failure of the Faran community to protect the monks of Sinai is probably more intelligible if the latter lived a fair distance from Faran.

In addition to what he says about Mount Sinai, the treatise of Ammonius is interesting to us because it shows that Raithu was regarded by some as the site of Biblical Elim. This is not stated explicitly, but it is implied when it is said that Raithu is a place where πηγαί εἰσιν ιβ' καὶ φοίνικες ἑβδομήκοντα κατὰ τὴν γραφήν · νῦν δὲ τῷ χρόνῳ πλεονάσαντες.[53] The γραφή is clearly Ex. 15: 27, where just this description is given of Elim. This view of the location of Elim also appears in Cosmas (see below, p. 43), and will have been based on the plentiful vegetation of et-Tur. But there was another tradition, found in Etheria and Antoninus, which placed Elim further north, presumably to fit better with its place as the second named stopping-place after the crossing of 'the sea'.

ETHERIA

The *Peregrinatio* of Etheria illustrates perfectly the contribution of pilgrimage to the growth of a developed system of identifications of the Biblical place-names.[54] It is a record of several journeys through the Holy Land and neighbouring regions by a Christian who emerges from the account as a person of intense devotion with a consuming interest in the holy places. The work survives in only one MS. and unfortunately both the beginning and the end are lost. The missing sections can in part be reconstructed from later works which made reference to them or used them. The most important of these are a letter of a seventh-century monk named Valerius, which also provides us with the name of the pilgrim,[55] and a work called *On Holy Places* by one Deacon Peter, an eleventh-century monk of Monte Cassino in Italy.[56] From sections where the latter's work, which itself does not survive in its entirety, parallels the extant portion of the *Peregrinatio*, it is evident that he used it as one of his sources and often reproduced its wording quite fully. With the help of Valerius' letter, which gives the contents of Etheria's account in outline, and by the elimination of material which certainly derives from another source (such as Bede), it is possible to isolate from Peter's work what seems to have been taken over from Etheria.

From the evidence of her account Etheria's pilgrimage can be dated with certainty between 363 and 540, and most scholars have preferred a date nearer to the earlier of these two limits. Recently it has been persuasively argued that it must have taken place in the years 381–4.[57]

Etheria made two journeys in which she visited places which were claimed to be referred to in the itineraries. In the course of a visit to Mount Nebo (*Peregrinatio* chs. 10–12) she saw what were said to be remains of the final Israelite encampment near Livias (10.4), and near the sixth milestone 'after' (i.e. east of) that city she was shown a spring where Moses was supposed to have given the Israelites water, presumably while they were encamped in the 'plains of Moab' (10.8–11.2).[58]

The other journey of Etheria with which we are concerned here preserves traditions of which Eusebius says nothing, either because they only came into existence after his time or because he was not in contact with the circles where they were passed on. These provided identifications of the places between Egypt and Mount Sinai and those immediately after Mount Sinai. The sites which Etheria visited can be at least approximately identified with the help of four places whose location is known: the city of Arabia in eastern Egypt (probably the same as Phacusa, modern Fakūs),[59] Hero/Heroopolis (at or near Tell el-Maskhuta),[60] Clysma (near modern Suez, where the name survives in the form Kōm Qulzum)[61] and Faran.

Rameses is said by Etheria to be 4 miles (6.4 km) from Arabia (8.1). It could therefore have been identified with Qantir,[62] although there is a difficulty in that it is not situated on the direct route from Heroopolis to Phacusa, which is where Etheria's words suggest that Rameses lay. For this reason Tell er-Retabe is perhaps to be preferred.[63] Etheria was also shown the reputed sites of Succoth and Etham (7.5), but her account does not permit us to say more than that they were between Heroopolis and Clysma. She also saw places identified with Pi-hahiroth (Epauleum), Migdol and Baal-zephon, but again her narrative is not precise. Her guides regarded Baal-zephon as the name of a plain above the Red Sea. Apparently the place of the crossing of the sea was described in more detail in the missing part of Etheria's work (cf. 'quem superius dixi' in 7.4) and her words can probably be recovered from Deacon Peter's *On Holy Places*. He describes the topography of the Exodus in some detail and clearly locates the plain of which Etheria speaks west of Suez, between it and 'the mountain' (Jebel Attaqa).[64] He also mentions what were held to be huge chariot tracks left by Pharaoh as he entered the dried-up sea in pursuit of the Israelites.[65] Since these are mentioned by Orosius, who wrote at the beginning of the fifth century, it is quite possible that they could have been seen by Etheria and included in her account. That it was indeed at Clysma that the Israelites crossed the sea is stated by Etheria herself (7.1).

For the next section of the route we are again dependent on what can be culled from Deacon Peter's work. He describes what lay along the route taken by Israel, and since he places Rephidim close to 'the village of Faran',[66] we can deduce that the places which he refers to were on the west coast route of the Sinai peninsula. One of these, Arandara, which he identifies with Elim,[67] is probably the oasis in Wadi Garandel, about 50 miles (80 km) from Suez, where the name is preserved with only a slight alteration. He also has definite places in mind for the Wilderness of Shur, Marah, the Wilderness of Sin and the encampment by the Red Sea after Elim.[68] Mount Sinai was 35 Roman miles (51 km) on from Faran[69] – this is the distance given in the *Peregrinatio* itself (6.1) – which takes one into the southern massif in which are located Jebel Musa and the monastery now known as St Catherine's.

At this point information from the *Peregrinatio* again becomes available. The interpretation of the details must proceed from the very exact indication which Etheria gives of the distance from Faran to Mount Sinai. According to H. Pétré: 'The distance from the present-day oasis of Feiran to the Sinai massif' – she means Jebel Musa – '(some fifty kilometres) corresponds well to that which Etheria indicates here.'[70] That Etheria did indeed mean Jebel Musa when she spoke of 'Sinai' or 'the mountain of God' is proved by the striking way in which her detailed description (*Peregrinatio* chs. 1–5) matches both the terrain and the ruins around it.[71] She appears to have approached Jebel Musa by the difficult route from the northwest, and left again by the same route, on which Kibroth-hattaavah was pointed out at a distance of four miles (6.4 km) from Mount Sinai (1.2).[72] This site is also mentioned by Deacon Peter, as is Hazeroth, which was presumably further down on the way to Faran.[73] From Faran Etheria says that it was a day's journey to 'the desert of Faran' (6.1), which must have been in the lower part of Wadi Feiran or in Wadi Mukattib. Since Etheria constantly says that she returned by the same way that she had come, and the outward route described by Deacon Peter seems to pass by the caves and inscriptions of Wadi Mukattib, this is probably the place meant.[74]

There then follows a most unexpected statement about the route of the Israelites.

The children of Israel also, on their way back from Sinai, the mountain of God, retraced their steps as far as the place where we came out of the mountains and rejoined the Red Sea... (6.3).

The idea that the Israelites visited Faran on the way from Sinai as well as passing near it on their way to Sinai has already been encountered in Eusebius' *Onomasticon* (and perhaps earlier – see above, p. 24). But why should one suppose that they retraced their steps as far as the Red Sea (i.e. the Gulf of Suez)? The answer is apparently that from the Wilderness of Paran (Num. 13: 3, 26) Israel was told by Yahweh to 'set out for the wilderness by the way to the Red Sea (יָם סוּף)' (Num. 14: 25 – cf. Dt. 1: 40; 2: 1). The 'Red Sea' here almost certainly refers to the Gulf of Akaba, but once the Wilderness of Paran had been located in the vicinity of Faran it is not difficult to see how it could have been thought to mean the Gulf of Suez. Etheria does not say where the Israelites went from this point (probably near Abu Zenima), but her language suggests that they took a different route from her after this, presumably turning inland again.

There are limitations in the topographical 'research' communicated to Etheria, which appear particularly serious in a case like this last one, where the fact that the spies were sent from and returned to Kadesh (Dt. 1: 19ff – but cf. Num. 13: 26 also) is completely ignored. But there is another side to this enterprise which deserves attention. Etheria's account reveals the sharp observation of the landscape which contributed to the fixing of the identifications that have been described. Although misdirected by unsatisfactory exegesis, this is an essential prerequisite for historical geography, as is demonstrated by its fine practice by more recent masters of the discipline such as George Adam Smith. No doubt the same fascination with the landscape played a part in some earlier identifications to which we have referred, but even so it is Etheria who is the first to communicate it so clearly to the modern reader.

COSMAS INDICOPLEUSTES

The following centuries seem not to have produced, to judge from extant literature, topographical works which treated the route of the Israelites in the same detail as the *Onomasticon* and the *Peregrinatio* of Etheria. Perhaps all that was possible had been achieved. But there are two sixth-century writings which witness to a continuing interest in some of the sites that have been mentioned.[75] The first of these is the fifth book of the *Christian Topography* of Cosmas Indicopleustes, which was written about 550.[76]

Although it has sometimes been doubted, Cosmas had certainly visited sites associated with the beginning of the wilderness journey.[77] He placed the crossing of the Red Sea at Clysma, and reported, like Deacon Peter, the alleged chariot-tracks of the Egyptians by the shore (sect. 8 = 196D). The place where the Israelites reached the opposite coast he calls Phoenicon (sect. 13 = 197D). No place near the north end of the Gulf of Suez with this name is known from other ancient sources, but it is probable that Uyun Musa is meant. The coastal plain to the south will then be Cosmas' Wilderness of Shur.

He gives no further identifications until that of Elim with Raithu (sect. 14 = 200A). Here he follows the tradition found also in Ammonius against that reported by Etheria (and Antoninus). It is probably a local tradition of the Raithu community. From Raithu (et-Tur) Cosmas says that the Israelites turned inland, and since they soon reach Rephidim at Faran he probably meant the route up Wadi Hibran. In connection with the 'water from the rock' episode (Ex. 17: 1–7) Cosmas says that Moses went εἰς Χωρὴβ τὸ ὄρος, τουτέστιν ἐν τῷ Σιναίῳ, ἐγγὺς ὄντι τῆς Φαρὰν ὡς ἀπὸ μιλίων ἕξ (sect. 16 = 200B). Mount Sinai at 6 miles (c. 9 km) from Faran cannot be Jebel Musa or one of the neighbouring peaks, which are over 30 miles (48 km) away. The figure does fit quite well the distance from the site of Faran to the imposing massif of Jebel Serbal (2070 m), and a number of scholars have therefore concluded that Cosmas' view (and presumably that of his local informants) about the location of Sinai/Horeb was different from that which is very clearly attested by Etheria and was later given official recognition by Justinian's building (below, p. 46).[78] But even though it is not out of the question that, say, the monks of Faran had their own local site for the sacred mountain, a closer examination of Cosmas' account suggests that he need not necessarily have been referring to Jebel Serbal at all.

The crucial words are ἐν τῷ Σιναίῳ. It appears that Cosmas used the longer Greek form of the name to refer not to an individual peak, but to the high southern massif of the peninsula as a whole. This is clearer in a passage in which he mentions the many rock-inscriptions in the area, which some Jews translated for him and explained as the work of the Israelites. After representing the forty years in the wilderness as in a quite literal sense the time of Israel's elementary education, since then they practised the art of writing learned on the holy mountain, he continues:

ὅθεν ἔστιν ἰδεῖν ἐν ἐκείνῃ τῇ ἐρήμῳ, λέγω δὴ τοῦ Σιναίου ὄρους ἐν πάσαις ταῖς καταπαύσεσιν, πάντας τοὺς λίθους... γεγραμμένους γράμμασιν....

(sect. 53 = 217A)

Both from the use of ἡ ἔρημος and from the mention of πάσαις ταῖς καταπαύσεσιν, it follows that τὸ Σίναιον ὄρος was a considerable area and not just a single peak.[79] The same is suggested by the passage which is our main concern, since it speaks of Horeb as being not identical to τὸ Σίναιον, but 'in' (ἐν) it. When Cosmas wants to speak of Mount Sinai in the narrow sense (the mountain of the law-giving), as he does when he continues his account of the Israelites' journey, he uses the form Σινά:

τρίτῳ δὲ μηνὶ ἦλθον εἰς τὸ ὄρος τὸ Σινά. (sect. 19 = 200D)[80]

Thus what he is in fact saying in section 16 is that Horeb is in the southern massif (τὸ Σίναιον), which does begin about six miles (c. 9 km) from Faran. He may not be saying that Horeb is the nearest point and so identical with Serbal, since ὄντι agrees not with Χωρήβ but with τῷ Σιναίῳ.[81] In any case, Cosmas nowhere says that Horeb and Sinai are identical. In this he reflects the general conception of the period that they were distinct.[82] Other sources imply that Horeb was quite close to Sinai, but do not agree over its exact identification.[83] This passage therefore gives no precise indication of where Cosmas thought Mount Sinai to be. Nor is his account of the law-giving itself of any greater help to us, since in it he makes no reference to place-names of his own time. But even though no positive conclusion is possible, it can be firmly stated that the evidence of Cosmas does not presuppose the existence of a tradition which located Mount Sinai in the narrow sense at any place other than Jebel Musa.

ANTONINUS PLACENTINUS

The other sixth-century writing which will be considered here is the *Itinerarium* of Antoninus of Placentia in Italy.[84] As the prologue makes clear, this was actually written by a companion of Antoninus, and it is more accurate to refer to it as *Itinerarium Anonymi Placentini*.[85] This has the additional advantage of preventing confusion with the much better known *Itinerarium Antonini*, the secular Roman road-book.[86]

Antoninus of Placentia made a grand tour of the holy places comparable to that of Etheria, in the course of which he visited 'Mount Sinai' and other sites connected with the wilderness journeys. The *Itinerarium* tells us that from Gaza he turned inland to Elusa (Halutsa) on the edge of the desert, and then came to a fort with a guest-house which was probably Nessana or Eboda (sects. 34–5). The journey from there to 'Mount Sinai' took him between 19 and 25 days – the relationship between some figures in the text is not certain. One day before reaching their objective the pilgrims came to 'locum ubi Moyses de petra eduxit aquas' (sect. 37). This looks like a reference to the Rephidim story (Ex. 17: 1–7) but when Antoninus' visit to Faran, which he regarded as the site of Rephidim, is mentioned later in the account (sect. 40), no hint is given that he was returning to a place which he had already visited on his outward journey. This suggests that a different place is meant in section 37, and the words 'locum ubi' could as well mean '*a* place where' as '*the* place where'. Jewish tradition early developed the idea that the rock from which water was drawn went through the desert with the Israelites, so that 'places where Moses drew water from the rock' could be identified in the wilderness even where there was no question of a location of one of the places named in the Bible in connection with the miracle. Probably this was the rationale behind the tradition reported to Etheria in the region of the final encampment in Transjordan.[87]

We know very little about Antoninus' route from Nessana to Mount Sinai. But it can be deduced from what is said in sections 39–40 about the choice of routes back from Mount Sinai, that he took neither the long route via Egypt nor the route via Aila and the eastern wadies of the peninsula.[88] He probably took one of the routes across Jebel et-Tih described by the explorer Edward Robinson,[89] and approached Jebel Musa from the north via Wadi esh-Sheikh. The 'place' may perhaps have been Abu Suweireh, a rather short day's journey north of Jebel Musa. As for Mount Sinai, there is decisive proof that for Antoninus it was Jebel Musa in the statement that beneath it lay 'monasterium circumdatum muris munitis', which can only be the fortified enclosure now known as St Catherine's Monastery, which was erected on the orders of Justinian (527–65) – the exact date is uncertain.[90]

From Jebel Musa Antoninus went on to Egypt, and the *Itinerarium* reveals the continuing popularity of three topographical traditions relating to the Exodus. The battle with Amalek at Rephidim is located at Faran, which has also come to be regarded as the site of Midian: the inhabitants claimed to be descendants of Jethro (sect. 40). Elim, with its 'seventy-two palm-trees[91] and twelve springs', is pointed out at a small fort called Surandala, quite likely another form of the name which survives in Wadi Garandel (cf. Deacon Peter's Arandara, also identified with Elim). The crossing of the sea is placed at Clysma, where not only chariot-tracks but the petrified weaponry of Pharaoh are said to be visible (sect. 41).

Finally Antoninus visited 'the city of Memphis and Antinous' (sect. 43), which was held to be Pharaoh's capital and the place from which the children of Israel set out, thus being identified with Rameses. The location of Rameses at Memphis on the west bank of the Nile south of Cairo implies a return to a view like that of Josephus (*AJ*) and the rejection of those which placed it in the vicinity of Phacusa (Etheria) or at Pelusium.

MAPS

We conclude our survey of early Christian tradition about the route of the Israelites by referring to two maps which mark some of the places or incidents mentioned in the wilderness narratives. One of these, the *Madeba map*, which was found as a mosaic floor of a sixth-century church in 1884, is by no means completely preserved and the whole south-eastern corner is missing. Moreover, the surviving part of the southern section of the map reveals severe distortions which are due to the artist's wish to include the Nile delta along with Palestine in his rectangular outline.[92] It is of course in this distorted southern section that most of the entries on the map occur which are relevant to our theme. Thus when the Wilderness of Sin and Rephidim are marked on the opposite side from Egypt of a long narrow mountain range which borders the Pelusiac arm of the Nile on the east, it cannot be assumed that these sites were adjacent to Egypt any more than that they were on the edge of the Negeb, which could also be inferred from the layout of the map.[93]

In accordance with Eusebius' *Onomasticon*, which was a major source for the information on the map, Hashmonah (Num. 33: 29–30) is identified with Azmon(ah) in Num. 34: 5, a place on the southern boundary of Canaan. The position given to it on the map, south-east of Elusa, may be intended to locate it near Ain Qadeis, in which case there seems to be contact with the tradition preserved in the Targum of Pseudo-Jonathan on Num. 34: 5, which renders Azmon by קיסם, probably an ancient form of the name of Ain el-Quseimeh, an important oasis near Ain Qadeis.

Due south of the Dead Sea is marked 'the wilderness where the Israelites were saved by the brazen serpent' (cf. Num. 21: 4–9). In the corresponding section of Num. 33 the name of Punon appears, which Eusebius, as we have seen (p. 34) located in just this area. It is probable that the situation of this entry on the Madeba map was due to a comparison of the Biblical accounts of the journey from Kadesh onwards. It has also been suggested that one or both of the vignettes across the Jordan from Jericho might have been intended to represent the places named in Num. 33: 49.[94] In view of the interest shown in the final encampment by other sources, this is not unlikely: but there is no text on the surviving part of the map to confirm it.

The other map, known as the *Tabula Peutingeriana* after one of its owners, is medieval in its extant form but generally agreed to be based on a much older original,[95] which has commonly been thought to date from the third or fourth century AD. Here too there is distortion, for the African and Levantine coasts form a more or less straight line. In the Sinai peninsula, which is considerably 'flattened' in its outline, two ranges of mountains are marked, one bordering on the Pelusiac arm of the Nile and the coast road to Palestine, the other in the peninsula proper and passed on its south side by a road. The latter mountain range is marked 'Mons Sina', and on the road appears 'Phara'. It has been supposed that the road marked is the route from Suez to Eilat and Akaba across the 'neck' of the peninsula (Darb el-Hajj).[96] The distances given on the map would support this view. But in the light of B. Rothenberg's discovery of a route of major importance through the south of the peninsula, taking in what is almost certain to be the site of ancient Faran,[97] it is very tempting to think that the distances are wrong – accuracy would be much more difficult to achieve (and preserve) in such an outlying area – and that the road on the *Tabula* is this more southerly route. The placing of Mount Sinai to the north of it would still be puzzling, as the route in question passes all the peaks usually envisaged as its site on the north. A relevant factor may have been that there would hardly have been room for the schematic mountain on the map south of the road, let alone the legend which notes that Israel received the law on Mount Sinai. The only other entry on the map which refers to the wilderness period is an inscription in red across the north of the Sinai peninsula, which reads: 'Desertum ubi quadraginta annis erraverunt filii Israel ducente Moyse.' This reflects the tradition, first clearly attested in Arabic sources (see Chapter 5), which led to the naming of this whole area as Badiet et-Tih, 'the desert of the wanderings'.[98]

ARABIC INTERPRETATIONS

Old Testament scholars have generally paid far less attention to Arabic geographical traditions than to those of Jews and Christians in trying to determine the route of the wilderness journeys. This is not surprising when the late date at which they are attested is remembered. Moreover, if the survey that follows (which is based only on what is conveniently available in the selections translated by Le Strange and Marmardji) gives a representative picture, there were remarkably few attempts to give a precise location to the places named in the Bible. Nevertheless, from the point of view of the history of interpretation this branch of the tradition is as important as any other.

The main exception to the general tendency of Old Testament scholars to neglect the Arabic evidence was A. von Gall. In the section on Sinai in his *Altisraelitische Kultstätten*,[1] von Gall cited a number of passages from the classical Arab geographers which, he claimed, supported his view that Mount Sinai was east rather than west of the Gulf of Akaba.[2] One of the tasks before us is to see whether von Gall has given an accurate picture of what Arab writers of the medieval period thought about the geography of the wanderings.

An appropriate starting-point is the definition of the area associated with the wilderness wanderings as a whole. The name Badiet et-Tih is given in nineteenth-century works to the whole limestone area of northern Sinai, but more recently its scope has been limited to the region south of the Suez–Akaba road below the 1000 m contour.[3] Two Arabic geographers of the tenth century gave a description of 'at-Tih, the desert of the children of Israel', which corresponds, it would appear, to the first of these usages. Istakhri wrote:

Its limits are the Jifar district on the one side and Mount Sinai and its district on the other. To the north of the Tih lie the outer limits of the Holy City and the other parts of Palestine; and its southern frontier is in the desert beyond the Rif district of Egypt, lying towards the Red Sea. (sect. 53)

According to Mukaddasi:

It is a place on the situation of which there is some discussion. The most reliable account is that it is the desert country lying between Syria and Egypt, which same is forty leagues across in every direction; everywhere are sand-tracts... The limits of this district are, on the one hand, the district of al-Jifar and on the other Mount Sinai; to the west the desert limit is conterminous with the Egyptian province of ar-Rif; and on the other side the Tih goes up to Syria. Through it lies the pilgrim road to Makkah. (sect. 179)[4]

The Jifar, mentioned by both writers, is the sandy coastal strip between Egypt and Palestine.[5] There can be no doubt that for them at-Tih was within what is now known as the Sinai peninsula. The same conclusion is demanded by the dimensions given by Mukaddasi, as from the border of Egypt to Aila is already about 150 miles (240 km), that is, rather in excess of 'forty leagues'. The last sentence of his account also indicates that an area north of the pilgrim-road (Suez–Akaba) was included.

It follows from this location of at-Tih that Mount Sinai was assumed by these authors to be in the south of the Sinai peninsula, for it appears as the opposite boundary to the Jifar region on the Mediterranean coast. This is fully in accordance with other passages, which refer to the existence of a Christian monastery at Mount Sinai, without doubt that known today as St Catherine's, below Jebel Musa. Thus Mukaddasi writes:

Tur Sina lies not far from the Bahr al Kulzum (the Red Sea). One goes up to it from a certain village called al-Amn, which same is the place where Moses and the children of Israel encamped. There are here twelve springs of fairly sweet water and thence up to Sinai is two days' march. The Christians have a monastery in Mount Sinai... (sect. 179)[6]

Further, according to Idrisi (twelfth century):

Jabal at-Tur is reached from Faran. (sect. 2)[7]

That Idrisi placed Faran in the Sinai peninsula is quite clear from the so-called 'Little Idrisi' map,[8] while Jabal at-Tur is just another of the Arab names for Mount Sinai.

The Christian tradition about the location of Mount Sinai was also known to Yakut, whose *Geographical Lexicon* was completed in 1225. He refers explicitly to the monastery, although he apparently confuses it with the church on the summit of Jebel Musa:

This monastery is also called the church of at-Tur. It stands on the summit of Mount Sinai, and is the place where the Fire shone forth to Moses before he lost consciousness. It is built of black stone, and stands on the flank of the mountain. The breadth of the walls is seven ells and it has three iron gates. To the west of it is a fine gate, before which a stone is set. This, when they wish, they can raise up. Thus, when any (enemy) arrives there, and is directed thereto, he finds the entrance shut. No one can then discover the place of the gate. Within the monastery is a spring of water, and there is also one outside. (2.675)[9]

Yet Yakut says elsewhere that there was an argument about the site of Sinai:

There is a difference of opinion on this subject. Some say that it is a mountain near Aila. For others it is a mountain in Syria. It is said that *Sina'* is the name of its rocks or its trees. (*Mushtarik* 297)[10]

The controversy was still alive a century later, as a passage from Abu'l-Fida shows (sect. 69).[11] It seems to be reflected in two successive paragraphs of Yakut's *Lexicon* (3.557–8).[12] In passing from the one to the other Yakut says:

But in the Nabataean language every mountain is called Tur and as soon as bushes and trees grow on it, it is named 'Tur Sina'.[13]

This is probably a citation of an argument employed in the controversy, for it implies that there are (or might be) many mountains called 'Tur Sina', and the Christians may not have lighted on the right one.

If this was a real controversy about the location of Mount Sinai, and not just a confusion arising from the disagreement among Arab writers about the southern boundary of Syria, then it is clear that a new identification, different from that main-

tained by the Christians, had been proposed between the
floruits of Mukaddasi, Istakhri and Idrisi and that of Yakut. For
the former group knew only the Christian tradition, but Yakut
is already aware of disagreement. This points to the second half
of the twelfth century or the beginning of the thirteenth
century. We may tentatively connect this new identification
with the breakdown of Moslem–Christian relations at the time
of the Crusades. Just as the Crusaders tended to group together
what they alleged were Biblical sites in the areas under their
control,[14] so the Arabs may well have looked for, and found,
reasons for doubting the topographical traditions so dear to the
Christians.

It is probable that the site favoured by the Christians is the
one said to be 'near Aila'. Since a popular route from Jerusalem
to Jebel Musa led via Aila,[15] it would be natural to say that
Jebel Musa was 'near Aila', especially after Faran ceased to be
occupied. The distance from Aila to Jebel Musa is no obstacle
to this view, as the southern tip of the Sinai peninsula, Ras Abu
Muhammad, was described as 'the cape that projects above
Ailah' by Idrisi (sect. 2). This means that the new identification of Mount Sinai was with 'a mountain in Syria'.[16] Which
part of Syria was envisaged in this variant topographical
tradition? A clue can be found in the passages which say that
Mount Sinai was in the vicinity of Midian.[17] It is quite clear
that the Arab geographers located Midian in the Arabian
peninsula, some east of the Gulf of Akaba, others further
south,[18] and so a Mount Sinai near to Midian would most
probably be in this region. The area east of the Gulf of Akaba
was considered part of Syria by some authorities,[19] and seems
the most likely place.

Old Arab traditions about the location of other places
mentioned in the wilderness itineraries seem to be few and far
between. Kadesh (in the form 'Kadas') does appear in a list of
'Israelitish towns in the desert districts of the Tih of the
children of Israel' given by Dimashki (sect. 213),[20] along with
Elusa, Beersheba and some others, but no exact indication of its
location appears. Faran was known as 'Faran of Aaron', for

some reason that is no longer apparent, to Idrisi, who described it as:

A district that lies forty miles from al-Kulzum and along the sea-coast. The city of Faran stands at the bottom of a gulf. It is a small town where certain of the Arabs of those parts have their camping-ground...According to the common saying, this is the sea wherein Pharaoh – Allah curse him! – was drowned. (sect. 2)[21]

Perhaps 'the district of Faran' extended some way up the coast, as Faran itself is much more than 40 miles (64 km) from al-Kulzum (by Suez). The drowning of Pharaoh was perhaps already at this time, as it certainly was later, associated with the place now known as Hammam Faraun, 'Pharaoh's Bath', near Wadi Garandel.[22]

A later tradition attested by Yakut distinguished Paran entirely from Faran in the Sinai peninsula and placed it in the Hejaz:

Faran is a Hebrew word turned into Arabic. It is mentioned in the Torah in these terms: 'God came from Sinai, he appeared from Sair and he manifested himself from Faran.' Sair, these are the mountains of Palestine, the place of the revelation of the gospel to Jesus. Faran is Mecca or its mountains, according to the witness of the Torah. His manifestation comes from there, it is his revelation of the Qoran to his messenger Muhammad. (3.834; cf. *Marasid* 2.328)[23]

Dt. 33: 2 is here seen as foretelling the rise of Christianity and Islam. Among the factors which made possible the application of the third clause to Muhammad in Arabia could well be the displacement of Sinai already noted. In any case it certainly represents another case of the transfer of a Biblical name from the Sinai peninsula to Arabia, and it too may have had a polemical origin and purpose in the period of the Crusades.

Two other places are connected by the Arab geographers with the wilderness journeys. One is Wadi Musa, the place known today as the site of the Nabataean capital Petra. The main entry for Wadi Musa in Yakut reads:

This wadi is called after Musa the son of Amran. It lies to the south of Jerusalem, between the Holy City and the Hejaz. It is a fine wadi, full of olive-trees, and is so called in memory of Moses, who came out of the desert of the Tih, leading the children of Israel with him. And Moses had with him the rock mentioned by Allah in the Quran (2.57) in the verse: 'And when Moses asked drink for his people, we said, "Strike the rock with thy rod", and from it there gushed twelve fountains.' And as he marched he carried this rock with him, and fared forth. And when he halted he threw it on the earth, then there would gush out from it twelve springs, according to the number of the tribes, so that each man knew his drinking-place. Now when Moses came to this wadi, and knew that his end was near at hand, he took thought for the rock and he fixed it on the mountain-side there. From it came forth twelve springs, which divided among twelve villages, a village for every one of the tribes. Then Moses died, but by his command the rock remained there. Now it has been related to me, Yakut, by the Kadi Jamal ad Din Hasan, that he saw the rock in this place, and that it is of the size of a goat's head, and there is nothing else on the mountain-side like to it. (4.879)[24]

This particular aetiological tradition, which relates to a rock probably of a different mineral composition from the dominant sandstone of the area, is a development of an older tradition which located Kadesh at Petra (cf. the Targumim) and specifically associated a certain rock with the episode recounted in Num. 20: 2–13 (cf. Eusebius). Although it is not stated outright that Moses died at Wadi Musa, this seems to be implied and, if it is, then the ancient site of Petra will have attracted to itself an event which was at an earlier period, more conformably to the Biblical narrative, associated with an area much further to the north.

Yakut also refers to Mount Hor (Tur Harun), the place where Aaron died according to the Priestly tradition, but he gives only the vague information that it lay 'to the south of Jerusalem' (3.559).[25] Masudi, a historian of the tenth century, is more exact, placing Aaron's burial place in Jabal Maab (Moab), 'among the mountains of the Sharah district, that lie in the direction of Sinai'.[26] The name esh-Shera survived until modern times as the name of the southern part of the Edomite plateau,[27] and the usage of the Arab geographers is in general the same.[28] It is probable that Masudi and Yakut reflect a view like that of Josephus before them and recent Arab tradition after them (cf. the modern Jebel Harun), to the effect that Mount Hor was close to Petra. Whether the same mountain was always thought of as Mount Hor is another matter, and we have noted above (pp. 33–4) a difficulty in the way of assuming that Jebel Harun was meant by Eusebius.

Thus in the Arab traditions from the Middle Ages about the places visited by the Israelites it is possible to distinguish an original base corresponding to and without doubt derived from the much fuller Jewish and Christian accounts, which was gradually supplemented and altered, under the influence of both local speculation and, in all probability, anti-Christian polemic. Yakut and later geographers show the results of this development much more strongly than the older sources, which means that it is misleading to do as von Gall did in his discussion of Mount Sinai and cite only the evidence of the later authors, as if they were truly representative of the whole Arab geographical tradition. This literature needs to be approached in a way which recognises fully its own inner history and the variety of topographical traditions which it may contain.

CHAPTER 6

BEHIND THE TRADITIONS

Since the discussion of early Jewish, Christian and Arabic tradition about the route of the Israelites has involved so much intricate examination of various literary sources, it may be helpful if, before proceeding further, we summarise our findings.

At the beginning of the history of the interpretation of the wilderness itineraries, so far as we can recover it, the Septuagint already indicates contemporary equivalents for places at the beginning of the journey. It equates Yam Suf with the Red Sea, and this remains basic for most later interpretations. The *Antiquities* of Josephus show how a more exact conception of the initial stages had emerged and how some important sites in the later part of the journey were beginning to be located, particularly in Transjordan. In *Contra Apionem* a markedly different tradition, which places the point of departure in the north-east of the Nile delta, appears, but there is nothing to suggest that Josephus took this to imply a divergent route further on. Elements in the Targumim which go back to the Tannaitic period or before presuppose the same northern point of departure and outline a route which passes into the desert east of Egypt and then reaches Mount Sinai in the south of the peninsula. Traditions in the Talmud and Midrash from the same period show that the final encampment in the plains of Moab was being pointed out to travellers, and imply a considerable interest in the location of other events in the wilderness narratives. We have suggested the hypothesis that pilgrimages by Jews to some of these places may lie behind some of the descriptions in Josephus and the increasing number of identifications itself. But alongside elements of this kind there are in both the Targumim and the other Jewish sources occasional identifications which belong to geographical fantasy and make no topographical sense.

Christian tradition does not show any awareness of this developing Biblical geography until the time of Eusebius of Caesarea. The equation of Yam Suf with the Red Sea is assumed in the New Testament, and Mount Sinai is vaguely located in 'Arabia', but that is all. A pseudonymous document of the third century appears to locate Mount Sinai in the south of Palestine. In Eusebius identifications are concentrated in three main areas: in southern Sinai (where Mount Sinai is located according to him), in southern Transjordan, particularly around Petra, and east and north-east of the Dead Sea. The most notable gap is the lack of any attempt to specify the direction taken from Rameses as far as Rephidim. By a confusion that is only possible in Greek Eusebius located Iyyehaabarim near Petra, and also identified Hashmonah (between Mount Sinai and Ezion-Geber) with a place on the southern border of Canaan. In the latter respect he was followed by the artist of the mosaic map of Madeba.

The early stages of the Israelites' route are very precisely marked out in the report of Etheria from the late fourth century, and it is clear that her informants conceived of the first part of the route in a quite different way from Josephus. Other sources from the fourth to the sixth centuries reveal variant locations for some places in the early part of the route, but the view that there was at this time a variant tradition about the location of Mount Sinai does not seem to be demanded by the evidence. Some of the Christian identifications were manifestly taken over from the Jews, in many cases they may have been, while for a few (particularly in the neighbourhood of the Mount Sinai monastic community) a Christian origin seems most likely. Our extant sources suggest the fourth century as the time of the most rapid assimilation and creation of topographical traditions.

In medieval Arabic sources the route of the wilderness journeys receives little detailed attention. The crossing of the sea is placed in the Gulf of Suez, perhaps some way from its head. The Christian identification of Mount Sinai with Jebel Musa, sealed by the construction of the monastery under Justinian, is first accepted without question but later, perhaps as a result of the Crusades, doubted in favour of a location in north-west Arabia. The 'wanderings' are throughout believed to have occupied the central part of the Sinai peninsula, with the Israelites emerging at Wadi Musa (Petra), in the region of which both Moses and Aaron are held to have died.

Throughout the period covered by this survey a large number of places, particularly between Mount Sinai and Kadesh, seem to have remained completely unidentified. This may be partly because of a very imperfect knowledge of the central parts of the Sinai peninsula at this time, but it also seems to be the case that interest was focused chiefly on the main narrative of Exodus and Numbers, with the long itinerary in Num. 33: 1–49 being generally ignored where topographical questions were involved. It was valued much more for the possibilities which it offered for the 'spiritual' interpretation of the wilderness journey.

THE NATURE OF THE WRITTEN SOURCES

Anyone who is aware of even a little of the vast literature dealing with the route of the Exodus and the wilderness journey cannot but tread warily when attempting to probe behind these traditional interpretations and trace the path of the Israelites (or rather the path which later generations thought that they had taken).[1] Here more than anywhere else in the study of the wilderness itineraries there is the danger of implying that we know more than we actually do.

Even prior to the widespread acceptance of the Graf–Wellhausen theory of Pentateuchal analysis, towards the end of the nineteenth century, many different geographical theories had been proposed. Since 1900 the possibilities have been increased by the acceptance by many scholars of the view that the compilation of a continuous itinerary (Num. 33: 1–49) was a late and artificial phenomenon in Israel's literary history, and by the realisation that the Pentateuch might, and in fact does, contain divergent presentations of at least some parts of the route through the desert.[2] Even if, as we believe, the first of these factors in twentieth-century scholarship is no longer relevant, there can be no disputing the second. Moreover, the lack of precise and independent ancient references to most of the places mentioned in the itineraries remains as much of a problem today as it was for older geographical studies.

In an area where theories are many just because the evidence is meagre, a sound and explicit methodology is essential. This means, in an exercise in historical geography, recognising both the important contributions which geography and archaeology can make and the character of the relevant written evidence itself. Contrary to what is sometimes asserted, there are not two alternative approaches which can be played off against one another, one basing itself in field studies and the other working with the results of literary analysis. A true understanding will only be reached by giving due attention to the results of both types of study. In particular, the approach to be adopted to the Biblical evidence needs careful definition. (Some principles of method on the geographical side will be noted at the beginning of the next two chapters.)

Since it is beyond the scope of this monograph to enter into an extended discussion of some very complex questions of literary criticism, it will be necessary here simply to state the conclusions to which detailed study of the wilderness itineraries has led us:[3]

(1) The itinerary-material cannot all be treated as deriving from the same source.

(2) The itinerary-notes in the main narrative which parallel Num. 33: 1–49 (apart from those belonging to P) are derived from the latter passage, so that its fuller list of names must form the basis for geographical study.

(3) The incorporation of the itinerary-notes into the main narrative is a stage in the composition of the Pentateuch which cannot be exactly dated but which appears likely to be due to a Deuteronomistic redactor.

(4) Since the link between the itinerary-notes and the

individual episodes is secondary, places named in them cannot be located with any confidence by reference to elements in the stories with which they are associated.

(5) In view of the literary form it should be assumed that the itineraries do describe routes, and are not just haphazard lists of places visited by the Israelites in the pre-settlement period.[4]

(6) The evidence of other examples of the genre suggests that itineraries, with few exceptions,[5] give a complete account of the route described.[6] Gaps greatly exceeding the distance that might normally be covered in a single day's travelling ought therefore not to be envisaged between successive camping-places that are mentioned,[7] except where the text gives positive support to such an idea. Thus both Ex. 15: 22 and Num. 33: 8 speak of a journey of three days (perhaps a round figure)[8] after the deliverance at the sea; and Num. 10: 33 also speaks of a journey of three days after the departure from Mount Sinai.[9]

One problem does however arise in the application of the final principle to Num. 33: 1–49. If Kadesh is located in the vicinity of Ain el-Qudeirat and Ezion-Geber at the head of the Gulf of Akaba, as is normally done, Num. 33: 36 understood according to the above principle implies that two adjacent encampments were some 90 miles (144 km) apart! This problem is not removed, even if it is alleviated, by the adoption of Noth's view that Kadesh and Mount Hor are secondary additions to the passage or by 'the Ewald transposition'.[10] Both these theories still leave stages of about 40 miles (64 km) between Ezion-Geber and Zalmonah and between Zalmonah and Punon (assuming that the latter is indeed the ancient equivalent of Khirbet Feinan), which is well above the normal figure for a day's journey in antiquity. Rather than abandon a generally valid principle of interpretation (and one which makes good sense of the end of Num. 33: 1–49, where there are the most certain identifications) because of this difficulty, it seems advisable to seek a special explanation for its failure at this point. One possibility suggested by the non-Israelite parallels is that a familiar section of route was only cursorily described.[11] Another is that a section of route already traversed was used again (in the opposite direction?) and not repeated.[12] A third is that when Num. 33: 1–49 was composed, this was done on the basis of two route-descriptions which indicated the stages of journeys (*a*) from Egypt to Ezion-Geber via (?) the southern Sinai peninsula;[13] (*b*) from Kadesh to southern Transjordan.[14]

The study of the traditions of interpretation in Jewish, Christian and Arabic sources, to which the preceding chapters were devoted, does not provide such a useful basis when treated critically. This is partly because of the time which elapsed between the composition of the itineraries and the earliest interpretations of them which are available to us, and partly because in many cases it can most naturally be supposed that the identifications offered were worked out on unsatisfactory principles rather than being the expression of an ancient tradition. Nevertheless, the geographical interpretations of the early and medieval periods have their uses. Sometimes they indicate that a name known in a modern Arabic form has been associated with a particular area since ancient times, as in the case of Feinan/Phainon (cf. Eusebius). Also, there are traditions about the location of some places of major importance which reach back to such an early period in Jewish tradition that they must be taken into account when an attempt is made to identify these places (Yam Suf; Mount Sinai; Kadesh/Mount Hor).

CHAPTER 7

KEY POINTS ON THE ROUTES

In the preceding chapter we indicated the attitudes which we propose to adopt to the Biblical text and the traditions of interpretation contained in Jewish, Christian and Arabic sources. In addition we shall be guided by the principles of toponymy as set out by Aharoni.[1] There are however special problems in the interpretation of the itineraries which need to be overcome if the routes described are to be identified with any degree of certainty at all. On the one hand a century and more of exploration has been unable to discover more than a handful of plausible equivalents for names in the itineraries, either in ancient texts or in recent Arabic nomenclature. But on the other hand, where possible survivals of the names do occur, there is often more than one such possibility.[2] Fortunately there are a few places which are mentioned not only in the itineraries but in other parts of the Old Testament as well, so that these can be identified with some confidence and can then serve as indicators of the general outline of the routes described. For example, there is no doubt that the places named in Num. 33: 45b–49 lay on a route running north to a point near the northern end of the Dead Sea.[3] That itinerary therefore has a fixed terminus. Other places whose identification is of programmatic significance are Mount Sinai (or the Wilderness of Sinai), Yam Suf and Kadesh. Although there has been controversy about the location of each of these, in which the interpretation of the itineraries has played a part, the fact that an identification of one of them has to satisfy the demands of several passages, rather than only one, makes the role which we propose to give them a methodologically necessary one.

MOUNT SINAI[4]

In the past century and a half about a dozen different peaks have been claimed to be 'the true Mount Sinai'. This is not, for the most part, a dispute about which of a group of neighbouring mountains was 'the mountain of the law', for the sites suggested lie in several widely separated areas. Many scholars, especially in the nineteenth century, have continued to uphold the traditional equation with Jebel Musa or a neighbouring peak.[5] A small group has favoured Jebel Serbal, some 20 miles (32 km) to the north-west, in the (mistaken) belief that it was viewed as Mount Sinai in the earliest Christian tradition that is preserved.[6] Others, chiefly on the continent in recent years, have pressed the claims of one of the now extinct volcanoes in north-west Arabia,[7] or another mountain in Edom or east of the Gulf of Akaba.[8] A smaller group, again predominantly on the continent, has sought a suitable mountain in the neighbourhood of Kadesh.[9] Most recently, an Israeli scholar has advocated the location of Mount Sinai about 40 miles (64 km) south-east of modern Suez.[10] In the face of such divergent opinions, it is not surprising that some have preferred to suspend judgement[11] or have concluded that the Old Testament evidence relates to more than one mountain.[12]

It is not possible here to discuss each of these views in detail, let alone all the arguments that have been put forward for or against them. We propose only to outline the arguments which seem to us to give the strongest support to each alternative area, and to indicate our reasons for favouring one of them.

The traditional view has in its favour not only the tradition itself, which we have shown to be older and more uniform than is usually acknowledged, but the evidence of sacral associations for the area in pre-Christian times,[13] and the important and quite precise data of Dt. 1:2: 'It is eleven days' journey from Horeb by the way of Mount Seir to Kadesh-Barnea.'[14] The interpretation of the itinerary in Num. 33:1–49 also played an important part in nineteenth-century statements of this view, but this cannot be given decisive importance in the present discussion, because it is precisely the interpretation of the itineraries which is at issue. Also the explorers of that period had no scruples about using the narratives connected with points on the route to support their case, but we have laid it down as a principle that this cannot be done. Despite the need for these qualifications of the older use of the itineraries, it remains true that the location of Mount Sinai in the south of the peninsula can give a plausible account of the route described by the itineraries.

Those who have argued for a more easterly location (in Edom or in Arabia) have relied mainly on the apparent proximity of Mount Sinai to Midian and the fact that in poetic passages, one at least being very early in origin, Sinai is mentioned in parallelism with such places as Seir, Edom and Teman (cf. Jud. 5: 4–5; Dt. 33: 2; and for a similar passage which does not explicitly mention Sinai, Hab. 3: 3). All of these places are supposed to be east of Wadi Arabah or the Gulf of Akaba, and so it is argued that Sinai must have been there too. In addition to these arguments some scholars have pointed to what they have seen as volcanic features in the Sinai-tradition,[15] which, if an original part of the tradition, require that Sinai be a volcano which has been active in historical times – and it seemed that only in the Arabian Hejaz could such volcanoes be found in the vicinity of Palestine. Recently H. Gese argued that Paul's argument in Gal. 4 implies that he (and his readers) thought that Sinai was in this region, but we have shown elsewhere that Gese makes unfounded assumptions about Jewish tradition in the first century AD and that no such abstruse background is needed to render Paul's argument intelligible.[16]

The older arguments are also open to criticism. It is not at all certain that the Midianites of the Old Testament lived only in the area east of the Gulf of Akaba, where the name 'Midian' appears from Roman times onwards.[17] In the narratives of Numbers (chs. 22 and 31) and Judges (chs. 6–8) they appear in the region of Moab and even west of the Jordan. This has understandably led some to conclude that the Midianites were 'a large Late Bronze Age league',[18] and 1 Ki. 11: 18 implies that in the early Israelite monarchy Midian was between Edom and Paran, the latter certainly being west of Wadi Arabah. Perhaps a material indicator of the Midianite homeland is to be found in the decorated pottery found east of the Gulf of Akaba, in Edom and on Jezirat Fara'un and now dated by its appearance at Timna to the Late Bronze Age.[19] When it is remembered that in Ex. 3: 1 and Num. 10: 30 Sinai is implied to be outside the Midianite homeland, the value of Midian as a pointer to the true location of Sinai is still further reduced.

The argument from the parallelism in the poetic passages is weakened by the fact that in two of them 'Paran' appears (Dt. 33: 2; Hab. 3: 3). If *this* region could be placed in parallel to places further to the east, why should the inclusion of 'Sinai' imply an easterly location for it? Seir too may well have lain west of Wadi Arabah.[20] The poets seem to have coupled together several names relating to the far south without worrying if not all the places were in exactly the same area. Here as elsewhere it is a mistake to assume that Hebrew poetic parallelism involves perfect synonymity between different stichoi.

The allegedly volcanic features of the Sinai-tradition have been much discussed, and not all scholars have been willing to concede that the descriptions are based on the phenomena of a volcanic eruption rather than those of a storm.[21] Yet it is hard to escape the conclusion that verses like Ex. 19: 18 and Dt. 4: 11 suggest a volcanic eruption. A better line of attack on this argument is offered by the use of apparently volcanic imagery to portray divine intervention in some psalms and prophetic passages (e.g. Ps. 18: 9; Mic. 1: 3–4). It can then be suggested that the imagery in the Sinai-tradition consists of 'conventional portrayals of a theophany, both in terms of an erupting volcano and a thunderstorm'.[22] If this interpretation is adopted, a difficulty still remains, for one has still to explain how Israelite poets acquired their knowledge of the phenomena of an eruption. No other settled people of the Levant, so far as we know, spoke of divine intervention in these terms: storm and earthquake were the normal evidence of a god's arrival in the literature of neighbouring peoples.[23] There would seem to be two possible ways of explaining the knowledge of volcanic phenomena in Israel. The imagery may indeed have been derived from the active volcanoes of the Hejaz, through the mediation either of traders who had witnessed it or, as is more likely in view of the religious significance given to it, of a tribal group such as the Midianites whose homeland included parts of Arabia neighbouring on the Hejaz, which exercised a strong influence on Israel's religion at an early period.[24] Alternatively – and this is a suggestion which needs further research to test it – it is possible that some of the lava-deposits of Jebel Hauran, Jebel Druze (the eastern limit of Bashan) and southern Transjordan are the result of eruptions in the historical period[25] and that either before or after the settlement in Canaan Israelite groups became aware of them.[26] The volcanic imagery in the Sinai-tradition therefore need not mean that Mount Sinai was in the Hejaz. Moreover, the distance from Kadesh of some 350 miles (560 km) can only be reconciled with the 'eleven days' journey' of Dt. 1:2 by assuming an improbably high rate of travel.

The main arguments used to support the view that Mount Sinai was close to Kadesh have been based on its proximity to Midian, its appearance in poetic passages alongside other names (especially in Dt. 33:2, which, according to the popular emendations based on LXX, actually refers to Kadesh) and a reading of Ex. 15–17 which finds in these chapters evidence that after the sea-crossing Israel went first to Kadesh and only then to Mount Sinai. More general arguments starting from the (alleged) importance of Kadesh for the Israelites and the assumption that they took the most direct route from Egypt to Canaan have also been employed.

At first sight this view appears very attractive. It can give a good account of the two main types of evidence held by other scholars to favour a (non-volcanic) mountain in Arabia, and it has the advantage that it does not make it necessary to adopt the view that the major events of the Exodus and Wilderness periods were spread over a large area. Its advocates have also claimed that it makes the best sense of the sequence of events in Exodus and Numbers, and even the indications of distance in the former book. They make use of an observation of Wellhausen's, which however led him to a quite different conclusion – that the Sinai-narrative had been secondarily inserted into a series of narratives which centred on Kadesh.[27] Wellhausen noted how the *content* of the narratives in Ex. 15–18 closely paralleled that of Num. 11 and 20, and also that there were expressions in both Ex. 15: 23–6 and in Ex. 17: 1–7 which could be taken to imply the *location* of the events described at Kadesh.[28] Israel's first objective on leaving Egypt was therefore Kadesh. Some have suggested that it was also Kadesh which lay at the end of the 'three days' journey into the wilderness' which Israel sought permission from Pharaoh to make (Ex. 3: 18; 5: 3; 8: 23). Mount Sinai, according to the narrative of Exodus thus understood, was approached not direct from Egypt but from Kadesh, and this (it is suggested) is most intelligible if it lay near to, and preferably east of, Kadesh.

Yet there are serious weaknesses in this approach to the evidence. It is dependent on deductions from geographical passages which do not point to any precise location (the poetic passages and those referring to Midian); on the unjustified assumption that prior to the introduction of the itinerary-notes the wilderness stories were arranged in a geographical order; on an exaggerated picture of the importance of Kadesh for the Israelites (very few episodes are actually located there);[29] and on a lack of awareness of its distance from Egypt (it is more like seven days' journey than three, at ancient rates of travel). In addition, a location for Sinai near Kadesh would conflict with the evidence of Dt. 1: 2, which puts an eleven-day journey between them, and of Dt. 1: 19, which speaks of a 'great and terrible wilderness' between them; and it could hardly give an intelligible account of the itinerary in Num. 33: 1–49, which even if the 'Ewald transposition'[30] is adopted has fourteen stations between the Wilderness of Sinai and Kadesh.

The recent suggestion that Mount Sinai was in the northwest of the Sinai peninsula can give a good explanation of two pieces of evidence which most other theories seem to ignore: the fact that a journey from Egypt to the mountain at which Moses received his commission can be described as a journey taking three days (Ex. 3: 18 – cf. verse 12); and Aaron's meeting of Moses at this very place as the latter was returning to Egypt from Midian (Ex. 4: 27). Both passages imply that 'the mountain of God' was much closer to Egypt than other theories have envisaged. It is also claimed that this theory is required both by the sequence of 'wildernesses' through which Israel passed according to Exodus and Numbers and by the wilderness itinerary as a whole. Particular significance is found in the name Jebel Sin Bisher, which it is suggested preserves the name 'Sinai' to this day.[31]

However there are some difficulties here too. The interpretation of the itinerary that is offered is based on several assumptions which take for granted the originality of its connection with the associated narratives and indeed its authenticity as a record of the Israelites' route. Thus it is assumed that the stations must be separated not by an ordinary day's travel but by the much smaller distance that a migrating band of nomads, complete with families and animals, would be able to cover in a day.[32] Even on this figure it is difficult in the extreme to fit the seven stages of the itinerary between Marah and the Wilderness of Sinai into the 30 miles (48 km) or so from Bir el-Murr to Jebel Sin Bisher, the equivalents proposed for these encampments. Identifications for the Wilderness of Sin and the Wilderness of Sinai are sought which have respectively high humidity (cf. the 'dew' of Ex. 16: 13) and resources for a year-long stay (cf. Ex. 19: 1 with Num. 10: 11 – both passages from P!). The rejection of other theories is frequently based on the same assumptions. In fact this theory too is unable to accommodate the relatively precise data of Dt. 1: 2 (except by an unjustifiably low estimate of the distance that might be covered in a day's travel).

Yet there are some elements in the tradition which do seem to require a location close to Egypt. It is perhaps significant that they are directly associated not with 'Mount Sinai' as such but with 'the mountain of God' (cf. Ex. 3: 1; 4: 27).[33] One of the most interesting developments in recent studies of Israel's pre-settlement traditions has been the isolation by Noth of a group of traditions related to 'the mountain of God (or gods?)' and the examination of them by some younger scholars.[34] Noth observed the contrast between these traditions (especially Ex. 18) and the Sinai-tradition proper, but was not confident that they referred to a mountain other than Sinai.[35] However in the passages cited above there is adequate evidence to make a distinction between the two mountains on geographical grounds. The 'mountain of God (or gods?)', which is associated not only with Moses but also with Aaron, Midian and the pilgrimage-feast (Ex. 10: 9) in the desert, and must have played a major if obscure role in the early history of Israel's religion, needs to be not far from Egypt and might be either in the region of Jebel Sin Bisher or further to the north-east (Jebel Yelleg?), where some scholars have wanted to locate Mount Sinai. An exact identification is quite out of the question, since the available evidence does not go into this kind of detail.

Mount Sinai however must be located much further to the south. If the 'mountain of God' is, as we have argued, a different place, then one of the objections most often raised against a location in the Sinai peninsula is removed. For it is the 'mountain of God' and not Mount Sinai which is associated with the Midianites.[36] We may therefore reasonably suppose that the traditional identification of Sinai with Jebel Musa, a peak in the southern massif of the peninsula, is approximately correct – the Old Testament evidence is not such as to confirm or disprove the claims of this particular peak.

Our conclusion that two different mountains, separated by a considerable distance, played an influential role in the early history of Israel's religion raises important questions about the latter which cannot be dealt with here. For our present purpose, the geographical interpretation of the itineraries, only the position of Mount Sinai, which determines that of the Wilderness of Sinai, need concern us.

YAM SUF

As the preceding chapters have shown, Jewish tradition from the LXX onwards and all works influenced by it have equated Yam Suf with ἡ ἐρυθρὰ θάλασσα, a Greek expression meaning 'the red sea' which referred not only to the gulf between Arabia and Africa which is still known by that name but also to other waters to the south and east, sometimes not very clearly defined.[37] There is no reason to doubt, though, that the LXX translators used this expression to refer specifically to the northern arms of the Red Sea, the Gulf of Suez and the Gulf of Akaba. 'Red Sea' is not however a translation of the Hebrew Yam Suf in the sense that the connotation of the latter term is reproduced by it. For the most part the early interpreters were content to ignore the meaning of the name. But the Bohairic version gave a rendering which associated 'Suf' with a kind of water plant: *phiom enshari* = 'the sea of the water plant Shari'.[38] And Jerome, when faced with the difficulty of explaining why, according to Num. 33: 10–11, the Israelites camped by Yam Suf some while after their sea-crossing, noted that 'Suf' might mean 'reeds' as well as 'red', and so Yam Suf could in this case refer to a lake in which reeds grew.[39]

Rashi is the earliest commentator known to us to have explained Yam Suf in this way in all its occurrences. In his comment on Ex. 13: 18 he says: '"Suf" means a swamp in which reeds grow, as (Ex. 2: 3), "She put it into the reeds".' This explanation was adopted by some nineteenth-century scholars in conjunction with the observations of great quantities of vegetation in the waters of the Gulfs of Suez and Akaba, to which 'Suf' was thought to apply.[40] But from 1875 onwards a new interpretation based on the same botanical kind of understanding of 'Suf' rapidly gained ground. In that year H. Brugsch published his lecture 'L'Exode et les Monuments Égyptiens'. Here he argued that 'the sea of weeds' (his translation of 'Yam Suf') could refer to an inland area, 'Suf' being the Semitic equivalent to the Egyptian *athu*, and referring to the rich vegetation which grows in and around the water brought down by the Nile flood. To judge from his text and the map at the end of it, Brugsch thought that the name Yam Suf could refer to a number of areas, including the Nile delta as a whole, Lake Sirbonis on the Mediterranean coast, the Bitter Lakes and even the Gulf of Suez.

This general approach to the term 'Yam Suf' has remained standard for most subsequent investigations of the route of the Exodus,[41] and very few recent scholars have expressed serious doubts about it.[42] It owes its attractiveness not only to the fact that, as Jerome and Rashi had already observed, the element 'Suf' of the name can be equated with the common noun סוּף, which occurs in three Old Testament passages (Ex. 2: 3, 5; Is. 19: 6; Jon. 2: 6) and clearly refers to some kind of vegetation, but to the discovery of a related word in Egyptian which means 'papyrus' (*twf(y)*).[43] If Yam Suf was a 'papyrus sea (or marsh)', then clearly it could not be part of the open sea, because papyrus is a freshwater plant. But it is precisely here that difficulties, generally ignored by those who favour it, arise for this view. For the one stretch of water to which the name 'Yam Suf' without any doubt whatsoever applied, the Gulf of Akaba, is part of the open sea and has no papyrus or 'reeds' growing in it.[44] Nor is it clear that the Hebrew word סוּף referred only to papyrus or reeds. This is certainly the natural meaning to give it in Ex. 2: 3, 5 and Is. 19: 6, in view of the contexts, but it is not at all suitable in Jon. 2: 6, where quite apart from the placing of the poem in the mouth of Jonah (which may well not be the purpose for which it was originally composed) the immediate context is clearly concerned with the sea and not with inland waters where reeds might grow (cf. verse 3). Here the context suggests that the word refers to vegetation growing in the sea in which a man might get entangled.

Should we then, with Noth, draw the conclusion that Yam Suf is always the Gulf of Akaba?[45] The great difficulty with this view is that it fails to give a plausible account of certain passages which imply that Yam Suf was near to Egypt. These are Ex. 10: 19, which speaks of locusts being driven out of

Egypt into Yam Suf, and the passages which equate the sea which the Israelites crossed with Yam Suf (Ex. 15: 4, 22; Dt. 11: 14; Jos. 2: 10; 4: 23; Ps. 106: 7, 9, 22; 136: 13, 15; Neh. 9: 9). One of the latter group of passages (Ps. 106: 7) explicitly places Yam Suf in Egypt, and it is hardly likely that the decisive event of liberation took place, or was thought to have taken place, at the Gulf of Akaba some 150 miles (240 km) away from the eastern border of Egypt.

We have therefore to envisage a somewhat wider use of 'Yam Suf' than Noth allowed. The main alternatives are that it was the name given to the Gulf of Suez (and the rest of the 'Red Sea'?) as well as to the Gulf of Akaba; and that it included some stretch of water in the general area of the isthmus of Suez.[46] The advantage of the former alternative (and it is a very significant one) is that the use of the name involves no greater ambiguity than the Greek or modern terms which refer to both gulfs (and to the sea of which they are the northerly extensions); whereas the second alternative would mean that the same name was used both for a stretch of water in the isthmus of Suez and for one at least of the gulfs of the Red Sea, which is not a usage paralleled in other geographical terms that refer to the region, nor is it a very probable one. The reason why the second alternative has been preferred despite this problem is that it has seemed to be necessary if the Biblical passages that refer to the deliverance at the sea are to be harmonised with each other and natural phenomena and names attested in north-east Egypt. Since some passages seem to point to a stretch of water further north than Suez, while others place the crossing at Yam Suf, scholars have tended to prefer an interpretation of the latter (one which can find some support in Egyptian texts)[47] which enables it too to be placed further north. Yet it may be doubted whether the need to harmonise the various types of evidence is great enough to outweigh the improbability of the same term having referred to such different stretches of water as the Gulf of Akaba and the lakes of the isthmus of Suez. It is a striking fact that both in Num. 33: 1–49, which is our major concern, and in the narrative of Ex. 14 the sea that was crossed, which is defined very precisely by other place-names, is not called 'Yam Suf' at all; in fact in Num. 33: 1–49 Yam Suf is only reached four stages later. It is not impossible that there were two traditions preserved in Israel about the place of the deliverance, one placing it at Yam Suf = the Gulf of Suez (which became the standard view in post-Biblical tradition) and the other situating it further north.[48]

It is even possible to explain how these two traditions may have developed without introducing the improbable idea of a Yam Suf which was separate from the Gulf of Akaba and the Gulf of Suez. One approach is to regard the more northerly location of 'the sea' as original and to explain the transference to the Gulf of Suez as being due to an initially mythical use of 'Yam Suf' in Ex. 15: 4, which was misunderstood as a reference to the ordinary sea of the same name.[49] Another possibility which deserves renewed consideration is that at the time of the deliverance at the sea (or at some later period when the 'Yam Suf' tradition arose) the Bitter Lakes, where many scholars would locate it on the basis of features other than the reference to 'Yam Suf', were continuous with the Gulf of Suez and so naturally known by the same name. Subsequently the land rose and the lakes were separated from the Gulf, and then it was more appropriate to refer to the place of the crossing as הים (which could mean 'the lake');[50] while the tradition of a crossing of Yam Suf, which was not completely suppressed, led to a new location of the event on the Gulf of Suez. The geological events assumed by this theory can be shown to have occurred by the evidence of rock-formations near Suez and around the Bitter Lakes;[51] but it has never been shown conclusively that the lakes were joined to the open sea in the historical period. Some scholars have claimed that the rising of the land assumed could not have taken place after the time of the Exodus because of the evidence of ancient buildings of that epoch close to the sea-shore at Tell el-Kheleifeh and Abu Zenima, which would have been under water if the theory were true.[52] But the discoveries that have been made are compatible with a lowering of the shore-level of up to two metres in the historical period, and this seems to be all that the proponents of the northerly extension of the Gulf of Suez envisage.[53] Moreover, both N. Glueck and B. Rothenberg hold that there has been such a change in the shore-level at the north end of the Gulf of Akaba.[54]

To conclude, we hold that the Old Testament evidence for the use of 'Yam Suf' is best explained by the view which makes it a relatively unambiguous geographical term, namely the view that it referred to the Gulfs of Suez and Akaba, but not to separate stretches of water further to the north. If this is so, the translation 'sea of reeds', popular as it is, cannot be retained, since reeds do not grow in either of the gulfs. Instead either 'Yam Suf' as a transliteration of the Hebrew or 'the Red Sea' as an indication of the modern term which most nearly corresponds to it should be used.[55]

KADESH

In view of the practically complete agreement at the present day about the site of Kadesh it is difficult to imagine that for much of the nineteenth century it was a subject of intense controversy. The discovery of Ain and Wadi Qadeis by E. R. Rowlands and the exhaustive discussions of E. H. Palmer and especially H. Clay Trumbull have all but driven the opposition from the floor.[56] But previous to this many suggestions were made, most of them, like the Jewish tradition which reaches back in all probability to the first century AD, placing Kadesh somewhere in Wadi Arabah.[57]

The location of Kadesh at or near Ain Qadeis, which preserves its name, is based on a number of quite separate Biblical references to Kadesh which all point to the same area.[58] The clearest indications are to be found in two passages in the patriarchal traditions which suggest that Kadesh was south of Beersheba on the inland route to Egypt, 'the way of Shur' (Gen. 16: 14; 20: 1); in the opening speech of Deuteronomy, where Kadesh-Barnea is in or by 'the hill-country of the Amorites' (Dt. 1: 19–20) and the base for the expedition of the

spies (1 : 23–5); and in the quite full description of the southern
boundary of the land of Canaan (Num. 34: 1–5; Jos. 15: 1–4).
The statement that Kadesh (and neighbouring Mount Hor)
was on the border of Edom (Num. 20: 16, 23) is not difficult
to reconcile with such a location, when it is recognised that
Edom exercised control in some sense over areas west of Wadi
Arabah.[59]

In this case we are compelled by the evidence of the Old
Testament itself to reject the traditional equation of Kadesh
with Petra. No fully satisfying explanation of how this mistaken
identification arose is available, but we have indicated above
(p. 17) some factors which may have been responsible.

CHAPTER 8

ROUTES IN
THE SINAI PENINSULA

The location of Mount Sinai in the south of the Sinai peninsula
and of Kadesh at or near Ain Qadeis, together with the identification of 'Yam Suf' as the Hebrew name for the Gulfs of
Akaba and Suez, defines the general area to which the wilderness itineraries refer as the Sinai peninsula. Before passing to
the detailed identification of the routes described it will be
useful to take note of roads linking the points already identified
which have been found practicable in the Biblical period and
since. In the Sinai peninsula, as in other difficult terrain, it is
not possible to travel by just any route: the physical features,
particularly the mountain areas and the escarpments, prescribe
certain routes from which all travellers have been bound to
choose. It is probable that when the attempt was made to
define the route taken by the Israelites through the desert use
was made of descriptions of routes, oral or written, which were
already employed by travellers.

Already in the Old Testament several routes are mentioned
by name in the peninsula, but there has not been total agreement on their identification.[1] It is even possible that the same
route may have had different names, the choice depending on
which way one was going.[2] For our present purpose it is not
necessary to become involved in this controversy, because the
scholars involved do not disagree about what routes were in use
but only about the names by which they were known. In what
follows we bring together the conclusions of modern historical
geographers and the reports of the famous explorer Edward
Robinson, who was able to obtain first-hand information about
Bedouin routes in the nineteenth century. Where possible we
draw attention to the use of routes in antiquity.[3]

In the north of the peninsula there are three major east–west routes:

(1) The coastal road from El Qantara to Gaza, which has always been the regular route connecting Egypt and Palestine. Its stages can be reconstructed for the Ancient Egyptian period, and also for the period of the Roman Empire.[4]

(2) The road from Ismailia to Beersheba, which passes close to the probable site of Kadesh. This is generally agreed to be the 'Way of Shur' of Gen. 16: 7.[5]

(3) The road from Suez to Eilat and Akaba which links the heads of the Gulfs of Suez and Akaba. In Arabic this is known as Darb el-Hajj, because it was the land route taken by pilgrims going from Egypt to Mecca. It is not certain if this route was in widespread use in antiquity.[6]

There are four more routes in the north which take an approximately north–south direction:

(4) and (5) Two branches from the Suez–Eilat road turn off at the Parker memorial (Palestine Grid 972941) and at Qalaat en-Nakhl to follow tributaries of Wadi el-Arish and eventually reach the Kadesh region.

(6) The route from Eilat and Akaba to the Kadesh region and onwards to Beersheba and/or Gaza. Formerly this route was probably an important trade-route.[7] Either this or a parallel route is marked on the *Tabula Peutingeriana*.[8] There is little doubt that this is the route, known as 'the way of Yam Suf', taken by the Israelites on leaving Kadesh according to Num. 21: 4 and Dt. 2: 1.

(7) The route from Eilat and Akaba through Wadi Arabah to the southern end of the Dead Sea, the 'way of the Arabah' of Dt. 2: 8.[9]

South of Darb el-Hajj there were further well-defined routes:

(8) The coastal road from Suez south along the eastern shore of the Gulf of Suez. This was used by Christian pilgrims such as Etheria and Antoninus, and may have served as an alternative means of access to the ancient Egyptian turquoise mines, which seem generally to have been reached by sea and a brief land journey inland.[10]

(9) The east–west route from Wadi Feiran to Dahab through the southern mountains (via Wadies esh-Sheikh and Zaǵara).

(10) The route from Wadi Feiran to Eilat via Wadies Saal and Watir, which was used by the Nabataeans and by Jewish and Christian pilgrims visiting the south of the peninsula, to judge from the inscriptions discovered by Rothenberg.[11]

(11) Various approaches to the southern massif from the north-west: the routes most commonly mentioned are those via Wadies Babaa/Shellal, Maǵara, and Feiran on the one hand and Wadi Tayiba, Debbet er-Ramle and Wadi Labwa on the other (the so-called 'southern' and 'northern' approaches respectively). The former of these apparently used by the early Christian pilgrims Etheria and Antoninus.

Finally Robinson lists several alternative routes from the Sinai monastery to Gaza.[12] In addition to his own route, which was a combination of a variant of (10) with (6), he mentions three main alternatives:

(12) A route keeping to the eastern part of the Wadi el-Arish system, which crosses Darb el-Hajj about 20 miles (32 km) east of Nakhl. This could be reached from the monastery by ascending the Tih escarpment by either the pass of Rakna (not far from Serabit el-Khadim) or that of Mureikha (due north of the monastery). According to Robinson (p. 293) the route via Naqb Mureikha was 'the one most commonly travelled by the Tawarah', i.e. the Bedouin of the southern mountains. It passed close to the site of Kadesh.

(13) A variant of this, which branched off near Darb el-Hajj to follow the western side of the Wadi el-Arish system.[13]

(14) A route which skirts the Tih escarpment on the east, passing by Wadies Zalaqa and Watir to cross Darb el-Hajj at Thamad, and continues almost due north to the Kadesh region and beyond.

CHAPTER 9

IDENTIFICATION OF
THE ROUTES DESCRIBED

It is now possible, in the context provided by the preceding chapters, to examine the primary wilderness itineraries (Num. 21: 12–20*; Num. 33: 1–49*; Dt. 10: 6–7; and the itinerary-notes of P)[1] one by one, in the hope of establishing the routes to which they refer. We begin with the fullest and longest text, Num. 33: 1–49*. The three points already used to define the general outline of the route can also serve to divide it into four sections which can be studied separately.

RAMESES–YAM SUF

The first two places in the itinerary (prior to Etham 'on the edge of the wilderness') are generally agreed to have been in the eastern Nile delta and have been located with considerable precision on the basis of apparent references to them in Egyptian texts. Rameses is usually taken to be identical with *Pr-rmśśw*, the Ramesside city in the delta, which most scholars now locate at Qantir or at the neighbouring site of Tanis (San el-Hajar).[2] An Egyptian equivalent also seems to exist for Succoth in *Tkw*, a name of an area in Wadi Tumilat which extends west from modern Ismailia, and just conceivably the Egyptian name for Tell el-Maskhuta there, to which 'Pithom' in Ex. 1: 11 is likely to refer.[3] But some scholars regard 'Succoth' as a true Semitic name meaning 'booths' (compare the place of this name in central Transjordan (Gen. 33: 17 etc.)),[4] in which case only its general location in the border area infiltrated by nomads can be fixed.

The position of Etham, the next station, is not at all clear. It has been suggested that it is the Hebrew form of the Egyptian

ḥtm = 'fort', either in the sense of an individual fort or in a
collective sense referring to a whole line of defences along more
or less the line of the modern Suez Canal – such as is usually
thought now to be meant by the pure Hebrew name 'Shur',
which appears to be an acceptable alternative to 'Etham' (cf.
Ex. 15: 22 with Num. 33: 8). It has been noted that Papyrus
Anastasi VI.55, 60 mentions a *ḥtm* of Seti-Merenptah in or at
Tkw, which might perhaps be the Etham of the itinerary;[5] and
also that the important border-fortress of Sile, a little to the
north, was given this description.[6] But there is a philological
difficulty with all these explanations, as the א of Hebrew
אתם is unlikely to be equivalent to Egyptian *ḥ*. Perhaps mis-
pronunciation could explain this, but it would be unwise to
make too much of this possibility and we must be content with
the information provided by the itinerary itself that Etham was
'on the edge of the wilderness'.

The next encampment, that immediately preceding the sea-
crossing, holds out the hope that it might be firmly located,
since it is defined by no less than three place-names as well as
the reference to 'the sea'. It gives in fact the most precise geographical information in the Old Testament about the place of
the deliverance. Yet even with these names to work from
scholars have been unable to agree where the itinerary located
the event. One group, in Germany apparently the majority,
has interpreted the names as referring to the region of Lake
Sirbonis, on the Mediterranean coast east of Port Said.[7]
Another, in which W. F. Albright has exercised considerable
influence, has associated them with a crossing of part of what is
now Lake Menzaleh, close to the northern part of the modern
Suez Canal.[8] A further group has favoured a stretch of water
further south in the isthmus of Suez, near to Lake Timsah or the
Bitter Lakes.[9] Since the introduction of Egyptological material
into the discussion the traditional site at the head of the Gulf of
Suez, which was still the main contender for most of the nineteenth
century, has received little support.[10] This disagreement is due
not so much to different approaches to the evidence as to the fact
that the evidence itself is capable of several interpretations.

Naturally the reference to 'the sea' is of little assistance by itself, especially as it could even mean 'the lake'.[11] Of the names two, Migdol and Baal-zephon, are of a type which could and did recur even within the relatively small area which comes into question when the location of the sea-crossing is discussed, and Pi-hahiroth has received no explanation that is so clearly correct as to exclude other possibilities. The most recent examination of all the available Egyptian evidence was published by Cazelles in 1955,[12] and this favoured interpretations of the names which would place the crossing at one of the northern lakes. But it is clear from evidence mentioned by Cazelles that identifications of the places which would permit a more southerly route are also possible.

The equation of the Migdol of Ex. 14: 2 and Num. 33: 7 with that mentioned in some prophetic passages (Jer. 44: 1; 46: 14; Ez. 29: 10; 30: 6 – the last two using it for the northern extremity of Egypt) and in the *Itinerarium Antonini* has always played an important part in theories of a northerly location for the sea-crossing, as it is probable that this was situated at Tell el-Her near the Mediterranean coast.[13] But the most natural reading of Papyrus Anastasi v.19–20 implies that there was a 'Migdol of Seti-Merneptah' further south, south even of Wadi Tumilat.[14] Furthermore, the Cairo papyrus 31169 includes in 3.20–3 four places called Migdol, which seem from their position in the list to be near Wadi Tumilat rather than on the Mediterranean coast. One of them is probably called 'of Baal-zaphon'.[15]

As for Baal-zephon, the possibility of its being Mount Casios on the Mediterranean coast was strengthened by the discovery in Ugaritic texts of the equivalence of Zaphon and Casios as names of the mountain Jebel el-Aqra.[16] Yet it remains a little uncertain whether the southern Mount Casios achieved its sanctification before the Greek period.[17] Even if it did, it is clear that it was not the only place in northern Egypt where Baal-zaphon was worshipped, so that the possibility of the name Baal-zephon's referring to another place cannot at all be excluded.[18]

Moreover there are certain difficulties involved in the

adoption of the identifications of Migdol and Baal-zephon advocated by Cazelles, especially if, as we have maintained, Num. 33: 1–49 is a coherent description of a route and not a compilation of elements of quite diverse origin. Firstly, Tell el-Her, the proposed site of Migdol, is about 30 miles (48 km) away from Ras Qasrun (Baal-zephon?), and hardly likely to have been employed as part of the description of the same encampment, when there were other names in the locality which could have been used.[19] Secondly, it is difficult for this interpretation to do justice to the 'turn back' mentioned in the itinerary (Ex. 14: 2; Num. 33: 7). Thirdly, the distance from Wadi Tumilat, where Succoth was probably situated, to Lake Sirbonis is about 90 miles (144 km), a very long distance for the two stages of the itinerary which have to correspond to it. Fourthly, such an interpretation of the route must take it right away from the possible sites of the Yam Suf encampment, which was reached four days after the sea-crossing according to the itinerary. On all these counts the location of the 'sea' in the isthmus itself makes for a more likely interpretation of the route as a whole. From the point of view of the distribution of the stages of the itinerary over the distance from Egypt to the southern mountains a location in the region of the Bitter Lakes appears most satisfactory.[20] To hold to the traditional site near Suez is no longer possible now that the beginning of the journey is fixed so far north by the locations adopted for Rameses and Succoth. Nor does it allow a plausible interpretation of the 'three days' spent traversing the Wilderness of Shur (Ex. 15: 22), which is certainly the desert east of the isthmus and not, as was once thought by proponents of the traditional location of 'the sea', the coastal plain bounded on the east by the 'wall' of Jebel er-Raha.

For the next part of the route there are, theoretically at least, two possibilities, as Yam Suf could be taken to refer either to the Gulf of Suez or to the Gulf of Akaba. The latter alternative is usually ignored, but it is a possibility which has two points in its favour. The first is the similarity between 'Elim', the name of the preceding station in the itinerary, and

'Elath/Eloth' at the head of the Gulf of Akaba, equivalent to 'Ezion-Geber' or the name of a site adjacent to it.[21] The second is the appearance in the Old Testament of two passages which speak of a journey to Yam Suf through the wilderness – Ex. 13: 18: 'God led the people round by the way of the wilderness toward Yam Suf'; Jud. 11: 16: 'When they came up from Egypt, Israel went through the wilderness to Yam Suf and came to Kadesh.' Is this wilderness that is mentioned the northern half of the Sinai peninsula, the traditional 'desert of the wanderings', and is Yam Suf in these passages the Gulf of Akaba?

A difficulty for an interpretation of the itinerary in such terms might be seen in the fact that it does not correspond to any of the normal routes in the peninsula listed above. But this need not be a serious objection, as route (3) – Darb el-Hajj – could have been followed from near its western end or even perhaps, after initial use of a parallel route through the Giddi pass, joined nearer to Nakhl.

The real objections to such a view are that it implies a most improbable approach to the south of the peninsula, where we have argued that the Wilderness of Sinai was situated, and that it necessitates very high figures for the first four or five days of travel after the 'sea' encampment, particularly if the identification of Elim with Elath/Eloth is adopted (nearly 40 miles (64 km) per day in this latter case). The arguments in its favour are also far from compelling. Those who identify Elim with Elath/Eloth pay insufficient attention to the different terminations of the names, which are against their referring to the same place; while Ex. 13: 18 and Jud. 11: 16 can be taken in other ways, for example as texts which use Yam Suf of the sea which was crossed, as the sea-crossing itself took place 'in the wilderness' according to some passages (cf. Ex. 14: 11–12).[22]

There is therefore good reason for taking 'Yam Suf' to refer to the Gulf of Suez, as has traditionally been done, and locating Marah and Elim on the coastal road (8). Elim, with its twelve springs and seventy palm trees, can very plausibly be identified with the oasis of Wadi Ġarandel, which is some 75 miles (120 km) from the Bitter Lakes, a reasonable distance for four days' journey.[23] Explorers have traditionally located Marah at Ain Hawara and the Yam Suf encampment at the mouth of Wadi Tayiba, but neither of these identifications is certain.[24]

YAM SUF–WILDERNESS OF SINAI

The fundamental problem in this section of the route is to determine whether the 'southern' or 'northern' approach to the interior of the peninsula is involved. One route representing each of these has already been noted under (11) above, but both of them have alternatives at least at the seaward end. In favour of a 'northern' approach it is pointed out that it can offer a very plausible location for the Wilderness of Sin in Debbet er-Ramle and that the apparent omission of any reference to the large oasis in Wadi Feiran is more intelligible if it was not on the route described. On the other hand, the 'southern' approach has at all times, ancient and modern, been the more popular as a through-route. None of the identifications proposed for places mentioned in this part of the itinerary is of any help in solving the problem, with the possible exception of the equation of Rephidim with Wadi Refayid, which is adjacent to a (more difficult) branch of the 'southern' approach and on the edge of the central massif. Of the others, the attempt to find a reference to *mafqat*, the Egyptian word for turquoise and the area in which it was mined in Sinai, in the name 'Dophkah' is misguided and in any case would not make a decision between the main alternatives possible, as the Egyptians mined turquoise at points adjacent to both 'northern' and 'southern' routes (Serabit el-Khadim; Wadi Maġara); while the suggestion that the name 'Alush' is preserved in Wadi el-'Esh has little to commend it from a philological point of view, even if the reading אליש of Sam. should be more original that that of MT.[25]

The exact location of the Wilderness of Sinai cannot be determined. Explorers from Robinson onwards commented on the appropriateness of the plain er-Raha below Ras es-Sufsafeh, the northern extension of Jebel Musa, as the site of the law-giving described in the Old Testament.[26] But we have specifically excluded from our geographical interpretation of the itinerary arguments based on the fuller narrative traditions (above pp. 59–60 (4)), and it is entirely possible that just as 'Mount Sinai' may like other phrases formed with הר denote the whole highland area so 'the Wilderness of Sinai' was a general term referring to the wadies in it. If this were so, and the itinerary was based on a knowledge of through-routes, then a part of Wadi esh-Sheikh would have a strong claim to be the location of the encampment in the Wilderness of Sinai.

WILDERNESS OF SINAI–KADESH

There are a number of possible routes from the southern mountains to the region where Kadesh is to be located (see above). If the rearrangement of names in the itinerary suggested by Ewald is accepted, one of the inland routes is probably meant. The only name which really makes greater precision possible is 'Hazeroth', which has since Burckhardt[27] been equated with the philologically equivalent Ain/Wadi Ḥuḍeirat,[28] about 40 miles (64 km) north-east of Jebel Musa. If this identification is correct – and some doubts must remain, as the Old Testament itself shows that חצר was a common element in desert names[29] – then route (10) linking up either with route (6) above Eilat or with route (14) in Wadi Watir would be a likely candidate.

If the order of the names in MT, Sam. and the ancient versions is retained, then the reference to Ezion-Geber (Num. 33: 35–6) becomes an important landmark for this section of the route. Other Old Testament evidence makes it clear that Ezion-Geber was on the coast of the Gulf of Akaba (cf. especially 1 Ki. 9: 26; 22: 48), which rules out the similarly named Ain Ġadyan about 20 miles (32 km) north of Eilat.[30] The evidence from Tell el-Kheleifeh (excavated by N. Glueck in 1938–40) shows conclusively that there was no substantial extension of the Gulf of Akaba northward in ancient times. It is at Tell el-Kheleifeh that Glueck and F. Frank before him proposed to locate Ezion-Geber.[31] The site is a plausible one for a trading-post used as a base for trade with South Arabia and the East (1 Ki. 9: 26) and the periods of its occupation are claimed to correspond to indications of the history of Ezion-Geber in the Old Testament. But little archaeological evidence of its having any connection with seaborne trade was found and there is no protection there for ships from the storms of the Gulf of Akaba.[32] For these and other reasons Rothenberg has recently revived the early suggestion of Schubert[33] that Ezion-Geber was the island of Jezirat Faraun which lies off the west coast of the Gulf a few miles south of its head.[34] He has shown that ancient routes pass close to the island, so that it is not to be regarded as 'off the beaten track'. Iron Age pottery was found there and a variety of structures including a well-built harbour on the landward side. Since some of the pottery was similar to the 'Midianite' pottery found associated with Egyptian mine-workings in the southern part of Wadi Arabah, Rothenberg argues that Jezirat Faraun was initially an Egyptian mining port.

Both Tell el-Kheleifeh and Jezirat Faraun fit the Old Testament references to Ezion-Geber tolerably well, and a choice between them is difficult. It is to be hoped that systematic excavation of the structures on Jezirat Faraun will soon be undertaken, as the additional evidence obtained might well serve to confirm or disprove Rothenberg's theory. For the present it may be observed that if 1 Ki. 9: 26 means that Ezion-Geber as well as Eloth was 'in the land of Edom', this would be a somewhat surprising statement to find made about the island of Jezirat Faraun, and would tend to favour the retention of Glueck's identification. Whichever theory is preferred, the MT order of names clearly brings the route to the Gulf of Akaba before Kadesh is reached.

A further indication of the MT conception of this section of the route is provided by the name Bene-jaakan, as Jaakan appears in 1 Chr. 1: 42 among the descendants of Seir. Seir is probably to be located in the southern Negeb, south of Arad.[35] As Bene-jaakan is mentioned in the itinerary before Ezion-Geber, MT implies that the route from the Wilderness of Sinai led first through the interior in the general direction of Kadesh, then south to Ezion-Geber, and then north-west again to Kadesh.[36] Other pointers to the route would exist if Hashmonah (Num. 33: 29–30) and Heshmon among the southernmost cities of Judah (Jos. 15: 27) were the same place, and if Rissah (Num. 33: 21–2) were identical with Rasa, on the route north-west from Aila/Eilat shown on the *Tabula Peutingeriana*.[37] But neither of these identifications is very secure.

Koenig's hypothesis

A quite different interpretation of the names between the Wilderness of Sinai and Kadesh has been put forward by J. Koenig in a series of articles and a recent book.[38] According to Koenig, the places named were on a pilgrimage route extending through the *harrat* or lava-fields of north-west Arabia to the now extinct volcano Hala'l-Bedr, about 75 miles (120 km) north-east of al-Wajh, which Koenig considers to be the real Mount Sinai. In his book (which is based on and illustrated by photographs taken on his behalf) descriptions are given of various structures and inscriptions at Hala'l-Bedr. One inscription ('la pièce archaïque') would be particularly important if Koenig's interpretation of the photograph could be accepted. He sees here drawings of a group of human figures surmounted by what appear to be cultic symbols and the word בעלין in an Arabian script.[39] Koenig takes this to mean 'by the Most High', and interprets the whole ensemble as symbolising the supersession of a local volcanic deity by a heavenly storm-god. But Koenig's deductions from the photographs, including this one, have been subjected to a penetrating critique by J. Pirenne,[40] who suggests that the 'figures' are only the result of natural erosion.[41]

Koenig's approach to the itinerary is a development of that of Noth,[42] but rather than excluding from consideration all names in Num. 33: 1–49 which also occur in the main narrative, Koenig distinguishes the names preceding the Wilderness of Sinai from those which come after it, and holds that the former group are a fragmentary itinerary and the latter a complete one,

87

both describing routes from the head of the Gulf of Akaba towards Hala'l-Bedr. This reading of the passage has received approval, though with qualifications, from H. Gese[43] and R. de Vaux,[44] but important criticisms of Noth's fundamental study have recently been made by B. Zuber.[45]

The following identifications are suggested for places between the Wilderness of Sinai and Kadesh:[46]

Wilderness of Sinai	Below Hala'l-Bedr
Kibroth-hattaavah	Rigm al-Fašed
Hazeroth	Ain al-Ḥaẓar
Rithmah	Retame
Rimmon-Perez	(a pass)
Libnah	Umm Leben
Rissah	Bir al-Qena'(?)
Kehelathah	(edge of plateau)
Mount Shepher	Jebel Harb/Jebel Debbaj
Haradah	al-Ḥarada
Makheloth	al-Malqaṭa
Tahath	*
Terah	*
Mithkah	al-Hadab massif(?)
Hashmonah	?
Moseroth	*
Bene-jaakan	*
Hor-haggidgad	Bir Jadid
Jotbathah	*
Abronah	?
Ezion-Geber	Tell el-Kheleifeh
Kadesh	Ain Qadeis/Qudeirat

All the names marked with an asterisk are regarded by Koenig, as they were by Noth, as interpolations into the basic list. Only so can places as far separated from Ezion-Geber as Haradah and Makheloth be given locations east of the Gulf of Akaba, as Koenig wants. It should also be noted that al-Malqaṭa is south of al-Ḥarada, so that Koenig has to suppose that Haradah and Makheloth, their equivalents (it is alleged) in the itinerary, were accidentally inverted. The names of Hashmonah and Abronah are also virtually eliminated from consideration, as they have in fact to be if a reasonable distance is to be left between the stations east of the Gulf of Akaba. Further south the suggested identifications of Makheloth, Mount Shepher, Rithmah and Hazeroth produce gaps of about 80 miles (128 km) between the first two but only about 10 miles (16 km) between the latter two. The itinerary is therefore by no means a 'neat fit' along the route proposed. The only point at which there is any real strength in Koenig's case (as far as the itinerary is concerned) is in the series of identifications for the places between the Wilderness of Sinai itself and Libnah, especially the three cases of closely corresponding names in the correct order. It cannot be denied that this is difficult to explain as a mere coincidence. Yet it could be that, as all the three names which are so closely paralleled in north-west Arabia are common desert names just because they refer to widespread features of the landscape (חצר = enclosure; רתם = broom-tree; לבן = white). In addition the route between the sites suggested is practically impassable, as A. Musil found,[47] and is not likely to have been in regular use either for pilgrimages to Hala'l-Bedr or for other purposes. There is a much easier approach to that mountain from the south-west along the route taken by T. E. Lawrence in May 1917.[48]

To conclude, Koenig's interpretation of the itinerary, while attractive in some details, involves some hypotheses which are not themselves well founded (the omission or neglect or inversion of names) and the use of a route which is to say the least improbable. As such it can hardly necessitate the revision of our earlier findings about the location of Mount Sinai, and if the view that Hala'l-Bedr played a role in the history (or prehistory) of Israel is to be accepted it will have to be on the basis of other evidence than this.

KADESH–'FROM BETH-JESHIMOTH
AS FAR AS ABEL-SHITTIM'

The beginning of this section of the route will of course be differently identified by those who accept the 'Ewald transposition' and by those who do not. In the former case a southerly route from Kadesh will be required in view of what has already been said about Bene-jaakan and especially Ezion-Geber. Route (6) or the parallel route used according to Aharoni's view during Roman times, which enters Wadi Arabah further north, is presumably meant.[49] From Ezion-Geber the route will have followed Wadi Arabah north to Khirbet Feinan, which can confidently be regarded, as it has been since early Christian times, as the site of Punon/Pinon. Zalmonah has been connected by some with Calamona of the *Notitia Dignitatum*.[50] But the correspondence of the צ to Latin C must make this equation highly improbable – Latin C, like Greek κ, usually corresponds to a Semitic Kaph or Qoph. In any case the exact position of Calamona is not known.[51] From Khirbet Feinan the route must have ascended to the Transjordan plateau and eventually have joined the 'royal road'. The identifications of places after Punon/Pinon in the itinerary were for the most part satisfactorily worked out by Noth.[52] The equation of Dibon (Num. 33: 45–6) with Dhiban is a very useful landmark in this section of the route. One must however take issue with Noth's location of Oboth at Ain el-Weibeh, which produces an inexplicable detour to the west after Punon/Pinon. It is necessary to locate Oboth to the north of Khirbet Feinan, on the way to Khirbet Ay, which seems to preserve the name of Iyyehaabarim, the next station in the itinerary. Various alternative possibilities have been noted; but they all suffer from some disadvantage, and no precise identification can be made.[53]

The MT sequence of names suggests a north-easterly route direct from Kadesh to Khirbet Feinan, passing probably down Wadi Fiqreh (Nahal Zin on Israeli maps). Aharoni has deduced from this and the request of Israel that they be allowed to pass through Edom by 'the King's Highway' that this route was an important branch of the north–south route through Transjordan.[54] But its use has not been established either from other texts or from archaeological evidence. For the section of route after Punon/Pinon the considerations noted above apply in this case also, with the difficulty of locating Oboth at Ain el-Weibeh being even greater.

On neither view is it possible to accept the tradition that Mount Hor was the ancient name for Jebel Harun, in view of the distance from the site of Kadesh, which immediately precedes it in the itinerary. This tradition could only be followed if Kadesh were identified with Wadi Musa/Petra (or some other site nearby). It is probably from such an identification of Kadesh that the tradition arose; and it was on the basis of it that some nineteenth-century scholars defended the location of Kadesh in Wadi Arabah or at Petra.[55] There can be no doubt that such a location is erroneous, and Mount Hor must have been somewhere in the area west of Wadi Arabah. Several suggestions have been made since this became apparent, but the most that can be said for them is that they are on possible routes leading from Kadesh, and quite close to there.[56]

OTHER WILDERNESS ITINERARIES

The other wilderness itineraries or itinerary-notes can be dealt with more briefly. The vagueness of the place-descriptions in P and their small number makes any precise identification of routes impossible. From 'the sea' P takes the Israelites to the Wilderness of Sinai, which must have been in the southern mountains of the Sinai peninsula; then to the Wilderness of Paran in the north of the peninsula (cf. 1 Ki. 11: 18; Num. 13: 3, 21, which show that it was an area south of what was considered the boundary of Canaan); then to (Meribath-) Kadesh in the Wilderness of Zin and Mount Hor; and finally to 'the plains of Moab beyond the Jordan at Jericho' by a route not specified. Although P is concerned to preserve the journey-aspect of the wilderness tradition, it does so with the bare minimum of detail.

The two remaining passages are detailed enough but deal only with short sections of route. Previous attempts to interpret Num. 21: 12–20* have started from the presumption that it describes a route passing through the desert to the east of Moab.[57] But the phrases on which this presumption is based are probably redactional additions to an older nucleus, which may have referred to a route further west. On neither view can exact locations for the encampments be fixed with any certainty at present.[58] The valleys of Zered and Arnon are probably Wadi Hasa and Wadi Mojib respectively, but only knowledge of the position of the following stations could fix the points at which they were crossed. It is precisely here that there is uncertainty. No particular well is obviously the site of Beer. The name of Nahaliel has been thought by some to be preserved in Wadi Enkheileh, the central stream of the Mojib wadi-system,[59] but this is hardly satisfactory, as a more northerly point seems to be required by the context. It is more plausible to see the name, which means 'valleys/wadies of God', as a reference to Wadi Zerqa Main, whose healing springs might well have been seen as a sign of divine presence or favour.[60] Bamoth could well be the same place as is otherwise known as Bamoth-Baal, with the divine name omitted (cf. Num. 22: 41; Jos. 13: 17). The latter was a height from which the Israelite encampment was supposed to be visible (Num. 22: 41), and so perhaps close to Mount Nebo. A place Beth-Bamoth is mentioned in the Mesha Inscription (Moabite Stone), and might also be the same as Bamoth in the itinerary.[61] But the context there gives no indication of its location. The identification of the final encampment in this short itinerary is complicated by the possibility that two different descriptions of it have been combined, and by textual problems.[62]

Dt. 10: 6–7, to judge from the reference to Beeroth Bene-jaakan, describes a journey through the region of Seir (1 Chr. 1: 42). The location of Jotbathah at Ain Gadyan can find support in the attestation of the name eṭ-Ṭaba in the neighbourhood and in the appropriateness of the Biblical description 'a land with brooks of water' to the place.[63] But it cannot be regarded as definite, and the other places mentioned in this fragment have not been satisfactorily identified. Some light could be expected from Num. 33: 1–49, where all four names occur together again, but all that really emerges from that passage is that these places were situated two to five days away from Ezion-Geber, probably in a northerly direction. This too is compatible with the location of Jotbathah at Ain Ġadyan, but other possibilities can be envisaged.

NOTES TO THE TEXT

Notes to Chapter 1

1 Cf. G. W. Coats, *CBQ* 34 (1972), 135–52, and G. I. Davies, *TB* 25 (1974) 46–81.

2 Ex. 12: 37a; 13: 20; 14: 2, 9; 15: 22–23a, 27; 16: 1; 17: 1; 19: 1–2; Num. 10: 12, 33a; 11: 35; 12: 16; 20: 1, 22; 21: 4a, 10–11; 22: 1; 25: 1.

3 There is some evidence that Jews of the Tannaitic period visited places connected with Israel's history on pilgrimage, cf. B. Ber. 54a, MK 26a; also the tales of Rabbah b. bar Hana (third century AD) in B. Bab. Bathr. 73b ff. and B. Erub. 55b; for a discussion of these passages see below pp. 14–15.

4 See P. S. Alexander, 'The Toponymy of the Targumim' (unpublished D.Phil. thesis, University of Oxford, 1974), pp. 13–15, 233.

5 For Philo see especially the *De Vita Mosis*, but also other passages listed in the index in vol. 10 of the Loeb edition. Naturally the Midrashim and Targumim contain much relevant matter, as does Rashi's commentary on the Pentateuch. Among Christians Origen (*Homiliae in Exodum, passim*; *Homiliae in Numeros* 27), Ambrose (*De XLII Mansionibus* and *Expositio Psalmi CXVIII*. 5) and Jerome (*Ep.* 78, *Ad Fabiolam*) laid the foundations on which later treatments were based. The medieval *Glossa Ordinaria* on Num. 33: 1–49 is made up entirely of extracts from the named writings of Origen and Jerome. For other references see J. de Vaulx, *Les Nombres*, Sources Bibliques (Paris, 1972), p. 381.

6 In modern times this is especially true of A. Servin, *BIE* 31 (1948–9), 315–55.

Notes to Chapter 2

1 This has already been noted for other traditional elements in Philo and Josephus: cf. J. Bowker, *The Targums and Rabbinic Judaism* (Cambridge, 1969), pp. 30 n. 1 (Philo) and 31–2 (Josephus).

2 Cf. Strabo, *Geography* 17.1.21, 30. The whole area of Egypt east of the Nile delta (including Heliopolis) was sometimes referred to as 'Arabia'.

3 E. Naville, *The Store-City of Pithom and the Route of the Exodus* (London, 1885), pp. 19f and Plate 11.

4 J. Schwartz noted that LXX also brings Heliopolis into the list of store-cities built by the Israelites (Ex. 1: 11), and suggested that both this and the identifications of the land and city of Goshen in LXX were due to

94

the influence of an Egyptian story taken by Jews in this part of the country to preserve a memory of their ancestors' Exodus from Egypt (*BIFAO* 49 (1950), 68–82, especially 78 ff). But the identifications could have suggested themselves for other reasons, and the inclusion of Heliopolis in Ex. 1: 11 could equally well be associated with the tradition, recorded by Josephus, that it was the place where Jacob and his family settled (see below, p. 8).

5　E. Hatch and H. A. Redpath, *A Concordance to the Septuagint* (Oxford, 1897), p. 508c.

6　F. Preisigke, *Wörterbuch der griechischen Papyrusurkunden* (Berlin, 1925–31), vol. 3, p. 294.

7　The context, however, does not make it clear whether Epauleum was a local name or one taken from Etheria's Old Latin Bible, which was a translation from the Greek. The use of the diminutive form is against the latter alternative, but it is also a problem for the view that Pihahiroth was still identified with the same place as it was in LXX.

8　On this question see below, pp. 70–4.

9　Cf. LXX at Ex. 6: 15; Jos. 5: 1, 12. It is presumably based on the wider use of Φοινίκη attested by Strabo, *Geography* 2.5.24.

10　For the former see *AJ* 3.299 (Καβρωθαβα for קברות התאוה, compared with LXX Μνήματα (τῆς) ἐπιθυμίας): for the latter see ibid. 4.100, where Josephus' μέγα πεδίον reflects the true meaning of (מואב) ערבת, as against the δυσμαὶ (Μωάβ) of LXX.

11　*AJ* 3.33; 2.184.

12　H. St J. Thackeray, *Josephus* (Loeb Classical Library), vol. 4, p. xii.

13　See especially D. Barthélemy, *Les devanciers d'Aquila*, *SVT* 10 (Leiden, 1963), and F. M. Cross, *HTR* 57 (1964), 281–99.

14　H. B. Swete, *Introduction to the Old Testament in Greek*, 2nd edn (Cambridge, 1902), p. 379. A possible example is *AJ* 2.277–8, where Josephus may have been using the expanded Greek text of Ex. 2: 22; on this see my paper summarised in *IOSCS Bulletin* 7 (1974), 22–3.

15　*Joseph and Asenath* 22.2–4 (ed. Philonenko) follows Gen. 47: 27 in placing Jacob's settlement in Goshen.

16　H. Gese, *Das Ferne und Nahe Wort: Festschrift Leonhard Rost*, *BZAW* 105 (Berlin, 1967), 89–91.

17　G. Ebers, *Durch Gosen zum Sinai*, 2nd edn (Leipzig, 1881), p. 424, followed by H. Holzinger, *Exodus* (Tübingen, 1900), p. 65, thought that Jebel Serbal was meant. The statement that Sinai was the highest mountain in its area and impossible to climb does not fit Jebel Musa.

18　This is a Hellenised form of (ה)רקם, the Semitic name of Petra. Eusebius has the more exact equivalent 'Αρκεμ as Josephus' reading, but this does not make it certain that Josephus wrote it. Below (4.161) he uses Ῥεκεμη.

19 In Pseudo-Jonathan on Num. 33: 36; 34: 3 'the Wilderness of Zin', where MT places Miriam's death (Num. 20: 1), is interpreted as a reference to the thorn-palms (צִינֵי) of a mountain, 'the mountain of iron', apparently in Transjordan (Josephus, *Bellum Judaicum* 4.454 – cf. Alexander, 'Toponymy', pp. 188 ff). Possibly this is the mountain to which Josephus was alluding here, though it seems more in keeping with Josephus' conception of this part of the journey to envisage a mountain west of Wadi Arabah being meant. A 'Mount Zin' is also introduced in the Bohairic version of Num. 20: 1.

20 M. Avi-Yonah, *Gazeteer of Roman Palestine*, Qedem Monographs, vol. 5 (Jerusalem, 1976), p. 25. One further site mentioned in the itineraries, Ezion-Geber, is given a quite precise location ('not far from the city of Aelana', near modern Akaba) in a different context (*AJ* 8.163).

21 On early Jewish pilgrimages see below, pp. 14–15.

22 But cf. J. G. Gager, *Moses in Greco-Roman Paganism*, SBL Monographs, vol. 16 (Nashville and New York, 1972), pp. 113–18.

23 According to J. Bright, *History of Israel* (London, 1960), p. 111, it was identical with later Rameses and located at Tanis. J. van Seters considered Qantir more likely (*The Hyksos: A New Investigation* (New Haven and London, 1966), pp. 127–51). The Austrian excavations at Tell el Daba, adjacent to Qantir, have now made it almost certain that it was the site of the Hyksos settlement (cf. M. Bietak, *Tell el Daba II* (Vienna, 1975)).

24 The Targum of Pseudo-Jonathan has a westerly route from Pelusium, since it identifies Pi-hahiroth with Tanis.

Notes to Chapter 3

1 There is even some evidence of the rejection of etymologising interpretations. Two Talmudic passages, B. Bek. 5b (the fuller account) and B. Sanh. 106a, relate a disagreement between two Tannaim, R. Eliezer and R. Joshua (probably of the second generation), over the meaning of the names Rephidim and Shittim. The same dispute is referred to in Mekhilta, Amalek 1 (Horowitz, pp. 177–8). In each case Eliezer maintains that the name is only a place-name.

2 For further discussion of the geography of the Targumim in recent years see A. Diez Macho, *SVT* 7 (1960), 228–9, M. McNamara, *Targum and Testament* (Shannon, 1972), pp. 190–205 and especially Alexander, 'Toponymy'.

3 I am indebted to Dr P. S. Alexander for drawing my attention to this text and pointing out its significance to me.

4 Cf. *The Jewish Encyclopedia* (New York and London, 1906), vol. 10, pp. 290–1.

5 Cf. B. Rothenberg and Y. Aharoni, *God's Wilderness* (London, 1961), pp. 85–6, B. Rothenberg, *PEQ* 102 (1970), 19–20 and A. Negev, *The Inscriptions of Wadi Haggag* (Jerusalem, 1977), pp. 61, 73–80. The date of the Hebrew inscriptions is still unclear: Rothenberg suggested a third–fourth century date, but Negev prefers (for reasons that are not compelling) to ascribe them to the fifth century or later (pp. 73 f). He accepts that they are the work of Jewish pilgrims but holds, against the evidence discussed above, that they only visited the holy places in Sinai after the Christian pilgrimages had begun (p. 79).

6 It is generally accepted today that the Peshitta to the Pentateuch is of Jewish origin and is related in some way to the Targumim (R. Le Déaut, *Introduction à la littérature targumique*, Part 1 (Rome, 1966), pp. 60–3, and S. R. Isenberg, *JBL* 90 (1971), 69–81). The correspondences noted below are further evidence of such a relationship. To them may be added the fact that differences between צ and the other Hebrew sibilants are reflected in the Peshitta (as in the transliteration of צין), which would not be the case if it were simply based on LXX, where all sibilants have to be represented by sigma.

7 See the complex diagrams in Le Déaut, *Littérature targumique*, pp. 98–100, 122, and the associated discussions; also Bowker, *Targums*, pp. 16–20.

8 Elsewhere, if the Hebrew has קדש ברנע, the Peshitta has the fuller form רקם דגיא (e.g. Dt. 1: 2), on which see my remarks in *VT* 22 (1972), 161–2. The Peshitta is not consistent in its equivalents for קדש, as in Num. 33: 36–7 it has merely transcribed the Hebrew name. This might of course be due to a secondary assimilation to either MT or LXX.

9 Cf. p. 95 n. 18.

10 *VT* 22 (1972), 162. Some support for this approach might lie in the fact, noted by F. Hommel (*Ethnologie und Geographie des Alten Orients* (Munich, 1926), p. 621), that LXX on Jos. 15: 3 appears to imply the existence of two places called Kadesh on the southern boundary of the land.

11 'Toponymy', pp. 198–9 (cf. pp. 189–190).

12 For further details see *VT* 22 (1972), 155–8.

13 Cf. Num. 21: 11–20; 33: 44, 47–8.

14 See *Encyclopaedia Judaica* (Jerusalem, 1971), vol. 6, cols. 690–1; Avi-Yonah, *Gazeteer*, p. 54.

15 The Neofiti MS. has פילוסופין ('philosophers') in Num. 33: 5, which is clearly secondary and perhaps no more than an accident. But it *may* reflect a spiritualising interpretation of the wilderness journey as a progression away from non-Jewish philosophy to enjoyment of the presence of God. It was along similar lines that some early Christians understood the text.

16 There is probably no connection with the place Tarngola of the Tannaitic Boundary Lists and the Palestinian Targum on Num. 34: 15,

as it is too far north to have had any connection with the wilderness journey. But note the curious treatment of Mount Hor in Pseudo-Jonathan (below, pp. 25–6).

17 *BDB*, p. 782; cf. L. Koehler, *ZDPV* 59 (1936), 193–5.

18 *Onomastica Sacra*, ed. P. de Lagarde, 2nd edn (Göttingen, 1887), pp. 224.44–6, 252.52–6.

19 Cf. Strabo, *Geography* 17.1.20 and Pliny, *Historia Naturalis* 5.64 for the Tanitic Nile. On the location of San el Hajar cf. J. Simons, *GTTOT*, p. 244.

20 Beshallach Per. 1 = Horowitz, p. 83. On the age of this midrash cf. Bowker, *Targums*, p. 70. The same view is found in Rashi's comment on Ex. 14: 2.

21 Other rabbinic sources, on the basis of a purely etymological argument, identify Alush with the Wilderness of Sin, where the manna was first given (e.g. Bereshit Rabbah 48).

22 The explanation given in the footnote on this passage in the Soncino edition of the Talmud.

23 See (e.g.) *IDB*, vol. 1, p. 785 ('presumably between 18 and 25 miles [29 and 40 km]'). My own extensive investigation of ancient and comparable modern evidence indicates a figure of this order: see my article, 'The Significance of Dt. 1: 2 for the Location of Mount Horeb', forthcoming in *PEQ*.

24 P. P. Levertoff, *Midrash Sifre on Numbers* (London, 1926), pp. 59, 62–3.

25 On its exact identification, other references to it and its developing importance in tradition see below, pp. 31–3, 43–6, 48.

26 On Etheria (or Egeria) see below, pp. 38–42. For the location of 'her' Mount Sinai at Jebel Musa cf. J. Wilkinson, *Egeria's Travels* (London, 1971), p. 213.

27 M. Harel, *Encyclopaedia Miqraith* (Jerusalem, 1964–), vol. 5, cols. 1021–2.

28 It is possible that the same material stood in the exemplar of the Neofiti MS., as the latter has an omission due to homoeoteleuton in the middle of the verse. The Jewish origin of the tradition is maintained by Y. Tsafrir, *Qadmoniot* 3 (1970), 3. On pagan sacral associations of the area see the works referred to below, p. 110 n. 13.

29 Cf. F.-M. Abel, *Géographie de la Palestine*, Études Bibliques (Paris, 1933–8), vol. 1, pp. 384–5.

30 On Josephus' reference to 'Mount Zin' see above, p. 11.

31 Also in the 'Fragmentary Targum' (Ginsburger, p. 116) on 20: 23. But in other respects this collection of quotations seems to echo Pseudo-Jonathan more than Targum Yerushalmi II (cf. the spelling תרנוגלא in the rendering of Num. 33: 35–6 (p. 117)), so it is scarcely independent here.

32 The location of its southern part is marked by Y. Aharoni and M. Avi-

Yonah, *The Macmillan Bible Atlas* (London and New York, 1968), map 3. But, as Strabo (*Geography* 11.12.2) makes clear, the Amanus extended much further to the north-east and the north-west.

33 For a brief discussion see Y. Aharoni, *The Land of the Bible* (London, 1966), p. 67.
34 Cf. Mekhilta, Wayyassa Per. 1 = Horowitz, pp. 152–3 (on Ex. 15: 22)
35 Pascha Per. 14 = Horowitz, pp. 47–8.
36 It could alternatively be regarded as an extreme application of the exegetical principle Gezerah Shawah.
37 Cf. above, p. 96 n. 1.
38 Beshallach Per. 1 = Horowitz, p. 83.
39 Bachodesh Per. 1 = Horowitz, pp. 203–4.
40 Cf. *Ep.* 78 (*Ad Fabiolam*).9.

Notes to Chapter 4

1 Cf. Pseudo-Scylax, *GGM* 1.80; Strabo, *Geography* 17.1.21; Pliny, *Historia Naturalis* 5.65; Procopius, *De Aedificiis* 5.8.
2 Gese has argued from the context that Paul thought Sinai to be near to el-Hejra/Medain Salih, in modern Arabia (*Das Ferne und Nahe Wort: Festschrift Leonhard Rost, BZAW* 105 (1967), pp. 91–3). But his theory is ill-founded and unnecessary: see my article in *VT* 22 (1972), 152–60.
3 *De montibus Sina et Sion* 3 (*PL* 4.991). Its Cyprianic authorship is doubtful, but it is dated before 240 AD; see B. Altaner and A. Stuiber, *Patrologie* (Freiburg, 1966), p. 177.
4 Cf. Ptolemy, *Geography* 5.16–17; also Abel, *Géographie*, vol. 2, pp. 162–4, and M. Noth, *ZDPV* 62 (1939), 125–44.
5 On this cf. Abel, *Géographie*, vol. 2, pp. 169–71.
6 Procopius, *De Aedificiis* 5.8, says that Justinian built the Mount Sinai monastery ἐν τῇ πάλαι μὲν Ἀραβίᾳ νῦν δὲ Παλαιστίνη τρίτη καλουμένη. For Jerome (*Liber de Situ et Nominibus Locorum Hebraicorum*, in *Onomastica Sacra*, ed. Lagarde, p. 120.25) Aila was 'in extremis finibus Palaestinae'. The parallel in Eusebius (Lagarde, p. 234.75) does not mention Palestine, but possibly ⟨Παλαιστίνης ὁρίοις⟩ has been lost after ἐσχάτοις by homoeoteleuton.
7 There is another surprising statement about Mount Sinai, which locates it 'in terra Damascena', in the *Historiae Philippicae* (36.14) of Pompeius Trogus, a Roman writer of the late first century BC. On this cf. Gager, *Moses*, pp. 48–56 (esp. 52), and G. I. Davies, *VT* 22 (1972), p. 153 n. 2. Possibly the idea arose from confusion of the names Sinai and Senir (the 'Amorite' name for Mount Hermon according to Dt. 3: 9): this is not incompatible with Gager's suggestion that 'local patriotism' may have been involved as well.
8 Cf. Wilkinson, *Egeria's Travels*, p. 10.

9 On these works see C. U. Wolf, *BA* 27 (1964), 66–96, J. Wilkinson, *RB* 81 (1974), 245–57, J. N. D. Kelly, *Jerome* (London, 1975), p. 155. In the following pages references are given to the pages of Lagarde's edition of the texts in *Onomastica Sacra*, 2nd edn, using the line-numeration given in his margin. Where no separate reference to Jerome is given, it can be assumed that he has no variant of geographical interest.

10 E.g. *Onom.* p. 274.78–9.

11 E.g. Rimmon-perez, Libnah, Rissah.

12 The latter is also the only Vulgate rendering which does more than transliterate a Hebrew name in the itineraries. Attention should be drawn to the discussion of the Yam Suf encampment after Elim in Jerome, *Ep.* 78.9, where he suggests that it may refer either to an inlet of *mare rubrum* or to a lake in which reeds grow. But it is a purely linguistic discussion.

13 An unimportant exception is Hashmonah (Num. 33: 29 f), which was identified with Azmon (Num. 34: 4–5) because in Greek the names appear in the same form (*Onom.* p. 236.58 f).

14 *Onom.* p. 287.64–6.

15 Cf. Rothenberg and Aharoni, *God's Wilderness*, p. 166; Rothenberg, *PEQ* 102 (1970), 20, 26. The claims made for an Iron II occupation need to be viewed with some scepticism, since, as Dr Z. Meshel of Tel Aviv has privately informed me, later exploration of the site failed to produce any indubitable examples of Iron Age pottery.

·16 The figure of three days for the time taken to reach Faran from Aila is rather low, as the distance is over 100 miles (160 km). It is possible that the mistake arose by the corruption of $F = 6$ into $\Gamma = 3$, when the numbers were represented by letters of the alphabet.

17 *Liber de Situ et Nominibus*, p. 155.31–2.

18 This is in fact confirmed by the final sentences of the *Onomasticon* entry, which clearly refer to Gen. 14: 6; 21: 21.

19 *Onom.* p. 280.86–9.

20 *Onom.* p. 289.40–1.

21 *Liber de Situ et Nominibus*, p. 146.25–6. By an addition to this entry Jerome underlined the proximity of Sinai/Horeb to Faran.

22 E.g. Ebers, *Durch Gosen zum Sinai*, pp. 424–5.

23 In addition to the texts which we shall discuss in detail, there are numerous other references to monks at Mount Sinai in the fourth century, some of them no doubt more legend than history: cf. D. J. Chitty, *The Desert a City* (Oxford, 1966), *passim*; R. Devréesse, *RB* 49 (1940), 205–23; and Tsafrir, *Qadmoniot* 3 (1970), 2–18. But there is no doubt that Julian Saba, the great Syrian ascetic, was there (Theodoret, *Historia Religiosa*, PG 82.1316 B–C; Ephraem Syrus, *Hymns to Julian Saba* 14, 19, 20, which, if not by Ephraem himself, derive from the first half

of the fifth century; cf. E. Beck, *CSCO*, Scriptores Syri, vols. 140–1 (Louvain, 1972)), apparently in the 360s, and the church which he built seems to be one of those seen by Etheria on Jebel Musa (*Peregrinatio* 3.5–7, 4.1–2).

24 *Onom.* p. 291.88 ff.

25 *Onom.* p. 270.4 ff.

26 *Onom.* p. 247.62–3.

27 *Onom.* p. 288.85–7.

28 *Onom.* p. 252.57–8.

29 Cf. P. Thomsen, *Loca Sancta* (Leipzig, 1907: repr. Hildesheim, 1966), p. 112; Avi-Yonah, *Gazetteer*, p. 89.

30 The entry appears at *Onom.* p. 235.8 ff.

31 *Onom.* p. 244.44–6, p. 252.52–6.

32 Ain Gadyan is too far away from the sea, *pace* Thomsen, *Loca Sancta*, p. 19.

33 *Onom.* p.235.13–17.

34 The garrisons are also mentioned in the *Notitia Dignitatum* (ed. O. Seeck), which dates from about 400 AD, 81.34 (cf. 82.35). Jerome misunderstood τὸ ἐξέχον, which with the following words was quoted by Eusebius from Num. 21: 13 LXX, taking it to mean 'which projects upwards', and so began his entry with the words: 'rupes quaedam in sublime porrecta', i.e. 'a rock projecting to a great height' (*Liber de Situ et Nominibus*, p.121.4). He also modified Eusebius' later remarks in such a way as to suggest that a particular valley was meant (ll. 6–8), no doubt to take more account of the Biblical references to a 'valley of the Arnon' (Dt. 2: 24, etc.).

35 *Onom.* p.274.82 ff. ἐπί with the genitive of a place can mean 'in' or 'by' (*LSJ*, p. 621). A possible site for Maschana is noted by Avi-Yonah, *Gazeteer*, p. 79.

36 *Onom.* pp. 277.91–2, 246.33 ff, 267.91–2. 'Ianna' is not found in MT or Sam., which both have הגיא, but it appears in a minority of LXX witnesses. ἰαννά seems to be the hexaplaric form (cf. the cursives a and x, and the marginal reading of v, which attributes the same form to Theodotion). The Syrohexaplar has יחנא, which in Syriac script could easily be a mistake for יננא. Other MSS. of LXX approximate to this reading, the most important among them being Codex Vaticanus, which has ἰανήν. Most MSS. have νάπην= MT. The minority reading may well represent a Hebrew text different from MT and is the *difficilior lectio*, as MT could easily have arisen through the influence of Dt. 3: 29, 34: 6. It deserves greater respect than it has had from textual critics.

37 *Onom.* p. 247.81–2; *Liber de Situ et Nominibus*, p. 137.9–11. Cf. Thomsen, *Loca Sancta*, p. 43, Avi-Yonah, *Gazeteer*, p. 39. On the true site of Bethjeshimoth see below, p. 118 n. 52.

38 *Onom.* p. 235.24.

39 Livias was named in honour of Augustus' wife Livia (cf. Josephus, *AJ* 18.27; *Onom.* p. 248.87–8; *Liber de Situ et Nominibus*, p. 137.16ff), but was known as Julias for a time in the first century AD (A. H. M. Jones, *The Cities of the Eastern Roman Provinces*, 2nd edn (Oxford, 1971), pp. 273–4). The identification with Tell er-Rame (Thomsen, *Loca Sancta*, p. 84; Abel, *Géographie*, vol. 2, p. 273; Avi-Yonah, *Gazeteer*, p. 75) has been doubted, but a recent survey by the Heshbon expedition indicated that the site has an appropriate history of occupation (cf. R. Boraas *et al.*, *AUSS* 13 (1975), 227). Tell Hesban has been excavated by a team from Andrews University: for preliminary reports see Boraas *et al.*, *AUSS* 7 (1969), 11 (1973), 13 (1975) and 14 (1976). On the road from Livias to Esebus cf. P. Thomsen, *ZDPV* 40 (1917), 67–8; S. D. Waterhouse and R. Ibach, *AUSS* 13 (1975), 217–28.

40 In another entry Eusebius locates them 'above Livias' (*Onom.* p. 288.2–4).

41 *Onom.* p. 236.46–8.

42 *Onom.* p. 247. 78–80.

43 *Onom.* p. 277.93–5. According to Eusebius 'Mount Abarim' was another name for the same place (*Onom.* p. 237.4–5). On the remains cf. S.J. Saller, *The Memorial of Moses on Mount Nebo* (Jerusalem, 1941) and S.J. Saller and B. Bagatti, *The Town of Nebo* (Jerusalem, 1949).

44 *Onom.* p. 283.1 ff.

45 *PL* 25.987. There is a variant reading 'eo' (sc. the Dead Sea), which is followed by Thomsen, *Loca Sancta*, p. 13. But in view of the importance of the sixth milestone from Livias for pilgrims it is more likely that the feminine form is original. The 'fountain', if not one of the immediately adjacent springs, may have been the famous spring 3 miles (5 km) to the south-east, still known as Ayun Musa and probably that shown to Etheria as the water which Moses brought from the rock: to judge from her account it was customary to turn off the road for this at 'the sixth milestone', apparently from Livias (*Peregrinatio* 10.8–11.2). See also n. 58 on p. 103.

46 Waterhouse and Ibach, *AUSS* 13 (1975), 223–4.

47 Text in *PG* 79.589–693. Recent studies have given good reason for thinking that the *Narrationes* were composed much later and are of no historical value: Devréesse, *RB* 49 (1940), 218–20, Chitty, *The Desert a City*, pp. 170–1, J. Henninger, *DBS*, vol. 6, cols. 475–80. That they give no support to the Serbal theory was already shown by S. Schiwietz, *Der Katholik*, 4th series, 38 (1908), 23–5.

48 It may be noted that Ptolemy referred to the southern promontory of the peninsula, Ras Abu Muhammad, which is about three times as far away from Faran as Jebel Musa is, as τὸ κατὰ Φαρὰν ἀκρωτήριον (*Geography* 5.17.1).

49 For the Greek text see *Illustrium Christi Martyrum Lecti Triumphi*, ed. F. Combefis (Paris, 1660), pp. 88–132; Syriac fragments were published, with an English translation of the whole work, by A. Smith Lewis, *The Forty Martyrs of the Sinai Desert and the Story of Eulogius*, Horae Semiticae 9 (Cambridge, 1912).

50 See Devréesse, *RB* 49 (1940), 205–23, who is followed by Chitty, *The Desert a City*. But Schiwietz, *Der Katholik*, 4th series, 38 (1908), 16–22, showed the appropriateness of the report to the years 373–8; cf. also H. Skrobucha, *Sinai* (ET London, 1966), pp. 20–7 (esp. p. 26).

51 Cf. Skrobucha, *Sinai*, p. 1; Tsafrir, *Qadmoniot* 3 (1970), 5.

52 M. Harel, *Masᶜe Sinai* (Tel Aviv, 1968), p. 250.

53 Combefis, *Illustrium Christi Martyrum Lecti Triumphi*, pp. 96 ff.

54 Text in *Itinera Hierosolymitana*, ed. P. Geyer, *CSEL* 39 (repr. New York and London, 1964), pp. 37–101; also *CCSL* vol. 175, pp. 27–90; ET with introduction and notes by Wilkinson, in *Egeria's Travels* (London, 1971); cf. also *Éthérie, Journal de voyage*, ed. H. Pétré, *SC* 21 (Paris, 1948).

55 ET by Wilkinson, *Egeria's Travels*, pp. 174–8. The name of the pilgrim is variously given in different MSS. of this letter, and Wilkinson gives reasons, albeit not conclusive ones, for thinking that it was 'Egeria' and not 'Etheria': cf. his Note A, pp. 235–6.

56 Text in Geyer, *Itinera*, pp. 105–21; ET in Wilkinson, *Egeria's Travels*, pp. 180–210.

57 For details of the evidence see Wilkinson, *Egeria's Travels*, pp. 237–9.

58 There is no reference to this in the Bible, the 'water' miracles being located at Rephidim and Kadesh. But in view of the post-Biblical tradition that one and the same spring accompanied the Israelites throughout their journeys (cf. 1 Cor. 10: 4, Pseudo-Philo 11.15 and the Targumim on Num. 21: 16–20), it is not surprising to find a 'Moses' spring' being pointed out at other points along the route. See also n. 45 on p. 102.

59 Wilkinson, *Egeria's Travels*, p. 216.

60 Cf. n. 3 (ch. 2) on p. 94.

61 Wilkinson, *Egeria's Travels*, p. 205 n. 5.

62 Ibid. p. 217.

63 Cf. Pétré, *Éthérie*, p. 40.

64 Y7–9 = Wilkinson, *Egeria's Travels*, pp. 206–7.

65 Y5 = ibid. p. 205. See also Orosius, *Historiae adversus Paganos* 1.10.17.

66 Y15 = ibid. p. 209.

67 Y12 = ibid. p. 208.

68 For suggested identifications see ibid. pp. 207–8.

69 Y16 = ibid. p. 209.

70 Pétré, *Éthérie*, p. 118n. (cf. p. 33).

71 M. J. Lagrange, *RB* 8 (1899), 392. For details see Wilkinson, *Egeria's*

Travels, pp. 213–16 and the map on p. 92. One feature to which it is difficult to find any equivalent in the area is the valley 'sixteen miles [26 km] long and four miles [6.4 km] wide', where the people were supposed to have camped while Moses ascended the mountain (*Peregrinatio* 2.2, 5.1, 3). Pétré suggests that Wadi ed-Deir may have been included as well as Wadi er-Raha (*Éthérie*, p. 98 n. 1), but Etheria may have been misled by some figures that she was given (so Wilkinson, *Egeria's Travels*, p. 213).

72 According to Wilkinson (ibid.) at the pass of Naqb el Hawa, where the road opens out into a wider valley, as Etheria says (1.1).

73 Y16–17 = ibid. pp. 209–10.

74 For the caves and inscriptions see Y14 = ibid. p. 208.

75 Three, if the few remarks of Theodosius, *De Situ Terrae Sanctae* 19, 27, are included. For the text of this work, cf. Geyer, *Itinera*, pp. 137–50. According to Altaner and Stuiber, *Patrologie*, p. 245, it dates from 520–30 AD. The many Christian inscriptions published by Negev and certain of the Nessana papyri (cf. Negev, *Inscriptions*, p. 72) are also of general relevance here.

76 *Cosmas Indicopleustès, Topographie chrétienne*, ed. W. Wolska-Conus, 3 vols., *SC* 141 (1968), 159 (1970) and 197 (1973). For the date cf. W. Wolska (-Conus), *La topographie chrétienne de Cosmas Indicopleustès* (Paris, 1962); Altaner and Stuiber, *Patrologie*, p. 517.

77 This is clearly stated in sect. 53 = 217A, where Cosmas says that he was shown inscriptions by Jewish guides. Hundreds of Semitic inscriptions, Hebrew as well as Nabataean, have been recorded in the Sinai peninsula in modern times: for some recent discoveries see Rothenberg, *PEQ* 102 (1970), 19–21, and Negev, *Inscriptions*.

78 Ebers, *Durch Gosen zum Sinai*, pp. 432–4; Harel, *Mas'e Sinai*, p. 250; Wolska-Conus, *Cosmas*, vol. 2, p. 31. Even Lagrange, who forcibly argued that all other patristic sources were at least compatible with a location of Mount Sinai at or near Jebel Musa, conceded the point in this case (*RB* 6 (1897), 129).

79 Σινά seems to have been used in this way in the sixth century: cf. Procopius, *De Aedificiis* 5.8. Cosmas avoids complete ambiguity by keeping this term for the individual peak (see below) and using τὸ Σίναιον (ὄρος) for the massif as a whole.

80 Schiwietz, *Der Katholik*, 4th series, 38 (1908), 26–8. The passage describing the continuation of the journey is omitted in the MS. employed by Montfaucon, which helps to explain how the mistaken interpretation of Cosmas arose. Users of the shorter text might readily assume that Cosmas placed the law-giving near to Faran. But the significant words are clearly attested in Codex Sinaiticus (on the MS. tradition see already E. O. Winstedt, *JTS* 8 (1907), 607–14).

81 Against Schiwietz, *Der Katholik*, 4th series, 38 (1908), 26 n. 3.

82 Eusebius, *Onom.* p. 289.40–1 (cf. above, pp. 32–3); Etheria, *Peregrinatio* 4.1–2; *Anonymi Placentini Itinerarium* (see below) 37, 39.

83 Etheria and Anonymus Placentinus represent different traditions: cf. Wilkinson, *Egeria's Travels*, p. 215.

84 Text in Geyer, *Itinera*, pp. 159–218 (two recensions), and *CCSL* 175, pp. 127–74. On the relevant sections cf. F. Mian, *VetChr* 9 (1972), 267–301 and Negev, *Inscriptions*, pp. 77 f.

85 Altaner and Stuiber, *Patrologie*, p. 245.

86 *Itineraria Romana*, ed. O. Cuntz, vol. 1 (Leipzig, 1929).

87 Cf. above, p. 39 with n. 58. Theodosius (*De Situ Terrae Sanctae* 19) seems also to know this tradition.

88 These were the normal routes according to Theodosius, ibid. 27. For 'Abila' in *Itin.* 40 read 'Ahila' (i.e. Aila) with Gildemeister.

89 See below, p. 78.

90 The evidence is both literary and archaeological: cf. Schiwietz, *Der Katholik*, 4th series, 38 (1908), pp. 11 ff, Skrobucha, *Sinai*, pp. 32 ff.

91 The number of palms is not that of the Biblical text, which has 'seventy'. It is due to the influence of the 'spiritual' interpretation which saw in these palms a symbol of the missionaries sent out by Jesus according to Luke 10.1 ff (so Origen, Ambrose and Jerome in the works referred to above, p. 94 n. 5). In that passage the MSS. are divided, some giving the number as 'seventy' and others (including some Old Latin MSS. and the Vulgate) giving it as 'seventy-two'. An author (or scribe) familiar with this latter reading and the spiritual interpretation of the itinerary might easily make the mistake of thinking that the Old Testament passages also had 'seventy-two', especially if he were working from memory. It is interesting that exactly this 'slip' is found in Origen's *Homily 27* on the book of Numbers, sect. 11, in the Latin translation which is all that survives.

92 For photographs, plans and discussion see R. T. O'Callaghan, *DBS*, vol. 5, cols. 627–704; M. Avi-Yonah, *The Madeba Mosaic Map* (Jerusalem, 1954); H. Donner and H. Cüppers, *ZDPV* 83 (1967), 1–33; and more briefly, V. R. Gold, *BA* 21 (1958), 50–71.

93 The mountain-range is generally assumed to be Mount Sinai: cf. Avi-Yonah, *The Madeba Mosaic Map* p. 75.

94 By Donner, *ZDPV* 83 (1967), pp. 22–3.

95 Cf. J. O. Thomson, *History of Ancient Geography* (Cambridge, 1948), pp. 379–81 (with references). A modern edition is that of K. Miller, *Die Peutingersche Tafel* (Stuttgart, 1929).

96 E. Sachsse, *ZDPV* 51 (1928), 265–8; Miller, *Die Peutingersche Tafel*, Tafel XI.

97 See the report in *PEQ* 102 (1970), 18–21.

98 One possible explanation of the Madeba map's placing the Wilderness of Sin and Rephidim so far 'north' would be that it was based on a map which, like the *Tabula*, marked twò mountain ranges between the Faran road and Egypt, and its author failed to retain the distinction between them.

Notes to Chapter 5

1 *BZAW* 3 (1898), pp. 1–22 (esp. pp. 12–13).

2 Another study of less relevance to the present inquiry is that of G. Hort, *Jewish Studies for G. Sicher* (Prague, 1955), pp. 81–93, in which she sought to argue, largely on the basis of Arabic sources, that Midian of the Old Testament was located not far north of al Wajh in Arabia, so that a location for Sinai in this region is required. Hort very usefully exhibits the multiplicity of claimants to the name 'Midian' in Arabic tradition, but the ambiguity of the much older references in Josephus and Ptolemy is not sufficiently recognised in her essay for her main argument to be convincing. Nevertheless, since tradition did, as she has shown, connect Moses with the region in question from the tenth century onwards (art. cit., p. 83), it is clear that modern reports of a 'cave of Moses' servants' in its mountainous hinterland (A. Musil, *The Northern Hegaz* (New York, 1926), p. 214) could be based on a tradition of considerable antiquity. A similar approach to Hort's has been taken by H. von Wissmann, *RE*, supp. vol. 12, cols. 525–52, but see on this below, p. 110 n. 17.

3 (*a*) E. H. Palmer, *The Desert of the Exodus* (Cambridge, 1871), pp. 284 ff;
(*b*) Harel, *Mas'e Sinai*, p. 19 and map facing p. 232.

4 The translations are those of G. Le Strange, *Palestine under the Moslems* (repr. Beirut, 1965: original edn 1890), p. 29.

5 Ibid. p. 30.

6 Ibid. p. 73. For further references to the monastery in Arabic sources cf. A. S. Marmardji, *Textes géographiques arabes sur la Palestine*, Études Bibliques (Paris, 1951), pp. 74 ff.

7 Le Strange, *Palestine*, p. 73.

8 Cf. K. Miller, *Mappae Arabicae* (Stuttgart, 1926–31), vol. 1, part 3.

9 Cf. Le Strange, *Palestine*, p. 435.

10 Marmardji, *Textes géographiques*, p. 135.

11 Cf. Le Strange, *Palestine*, pp. 72–3.

12 Cf. ibid. p. 73 (557), Marmardji, *Textes géographiques*, p. 135 (558). The two views also seem to have appeared side by side in the Maraṣid (a revision of Yakut's work, made about 1300), 2.214–15.

13 This section is translated by von Gall, *Altisraelitische Kultstätten*, p. 12.

14 For the Crusaders' revision of Biblical geography see A. Saarisalo, *Arabic Tradition and Topographical Research*, Studia Orientalia XVII: 3 (Helsinki, 1952), p. 10 n. 2.

15 Cf. above p. 46 and p. 105 n. 88.

16 In Abu'l Fida's reference to the controversy it is a matter of '*the* mountain near Aila' (the well-known one?) but '*a* mountain in Syria' (a less familiar place?), which could be taken as confirming our view, if the translation can be relied upon in these details.

17 Yakut 3.557; Maraṣid 2.214.

18 A full discussion of the evidence is given by Hort, *Jewish Studies*.

19 Cf. Marmardji, *Textes géographiques*, pp. 50–3.

20 Le Strange, *Palestine*, p. 30.

21 Ibid. p. 440.

22 For the later tradition cf. Palmer, *The Desert of the Exodus*, pp. 240–1.

23 Marmardji, *Textes géographiques*, p. 159.

24 Le Strange, *Palestine*, pp. 548–9. Another passage of Yakut (3.332), translated by Le Strange (p. 536), makes the location of Wadi Musa clearer by placing it near to Shobek.

25 Cf. ibid. pp. 73–4.

26 Ibid.

27 Cf. G. Adam Smith, *The Historical Geography of the Holy Land*, 25th edn (London, 1931), p. 366.

28 For some relevant passages cf. Le Strange, *Palestine*, p. 35.

Notes to Chapter 6

1 On attempts to locate the place of the sea-crossing see H. Cazelles, *RB* 62 (1955), 321–32, C. de Wit, *The Date and Route of the Exodus* (London, 1960), pp. 12–20 (with map), Harel, *Mas'e Sinai*, pp. 90–117. On the identifications suggested for Mount Sinai see E. Oberhummer, *Mitteilungen der KK. Geog. Gesellschaft in Wien* 54 (1911), 628–41 (ET in *Annual Report of the Smithsonian Institution, 1912* (Washington, 1913), pp. 669–77), Harel, *Mas'e Sinai*, pp. 118–90, and especially R. de Vaux, *Histoire ancienne d'Israel*, Études Bibliques (Paris, 1971), vol. 1, pp. 398–410. Treatments of the rest of the route have not been recently surveyed: on the extensive earlier literature see Lagrange, *RB* 9 (1900), 63–86, 273–87, 443–9, and the commentaries of A. Dillmann and B. Baentsch on Exodus and Numbers.

2 On this latter point see M. Noth, *Festschrift für O. Eissfeldt*, ed. J. Fueck (Halle, 1947), pp. 181–90, Cazelles, *RB* 62 (1955), 360–4, M. Haran, *Tequfot uMosadot baMiqra* (Tel Aviv, 1972), pp. 37–76 (cf. *IDB(S)*, pp. 308–10).

3 For their justification see Part 1 of my dissertation, 'The Wilderness Itineraries in the Old Testament' (unpublished Ph.D. dissertation, University of Cambridge, 1975). I hope to publish a revised version of this in the near future.

4 A distinction must be made between what these texts say – that Israel

followed certain routes on her way from Egypt to Canaan – and what may have been the historical reality of her pre-settlement existence – a semi-nomadic way of life in the desert south and east of Canaan? On the latter see S. Herrmann, *A History of Israel* (ET London, 1975), ch. 3 (Gn edn, pp. 97–115) and for Egyptian references to groups in these areas see R. Giveon, *Les bédouins shosou des documents égyptiens* (Leiden, 1971), with the review of M. Weippert, *Biblica* 55 (1974), 265–80, 427–33.

5 Omissions occur (*a*) in well-known sections of route (cf. copy B of the Old Babylonian Itinerary); (*b*) in the secondary use of annalistic texts (cf. my account in *TB* 25 (1974), 53, 56–8, with bibliography).

6 Against H. C. Trumbull, *Kadesh–Barnea* (London, 1884), p. 145.

7 Cf. above, p. 23, with n. 23.

8 On the significance of the number 'three' cf. J. B. Bauer, *Biblica* 39 (1958), 354–5, and J. B. Segal, *JSS* 10 (1965), 14–15.

9 This note of departure from Mount Sinai is of separate origin from the itinerary-notes introduced from Num. 33: 1–49, and should therefore not be used to establish the distance from Sinai to the next station mentioned, Kibroth-hattaavah (Num. 11: 34–5).

10 On these see M. Noth, *PJB* 36 (1940), 5–28; H. Ewald, *Geschichte des Volkes Israel*, 3rd edn (Göttingen, 1864–8), vol. 2, pp. 283–5 (esp. p. 285 n. 2). Ewald was apparently the first to suggest that Num. 33: 36b–41a stood originally after v. 30a.

11 See above, n. 5. Israelite traders would have used the routes to Ezion-Geber, at least when it was in Israelite hands: on its history see N. Glueck, in *Archaeology and Old Testament Study*, ed. D. Winton Thomas (Oxford, 1967), pp. 440–3, and *The Other Side of the Jordan*, revised edn (Cambridge, Mass., 1970), ch. 4; also Z. Meshel, 'History of the Negev in the time of the Kings of Judah' (Heb.) (unpublished Ph.D. dissertation, Tel Aviv University, 1974), ch. F. There has been some controversy over the identification of Ezion-Geber with Tell el Kheleifeh (see pp. 85–6), but it still seems the most likely site. The use of the route from Kadesh to the head of the Gulf of Akaba by Israelites of the monarchy period has now been vividly demonstrated by Meshel's excavations at Kuntilat Ajrud (see below, p. 114 n. 7).

12 So H. Holzinger, *Numeri* (Tübingen, 1903), p. 163.

13 A plausible *Sitz im Leben* for such a route description might be found in Egyptian mining-expeditions to the southern part of Wadi Arabah, which appear sometimes to have used a land route: cf. B. Rothenberg, *Timna: Valley of the Biblical Copper Mines* (London, 1972), p. 201.

14 De Vaux thought that such a document might have been available (*Histoire*, vol. 1, p. 520); Y. Aharoni suggested that the route was a southern branch of 'the King's Highway' (Num. 20: 17), *Land of the Bible*, pp. 51–2.

Notes to Chapter 7

1 See *Land of the Bible*, ch. 6.
2 This is not surprising, as many place-names refer to features of the locality, which also occur in other districts.
3 Noth, *PJB* 36 (1940), 10–14.
4 For its importance in determining the routes taken see D. Baly, *Geographical Companion to the Bible* (London, 1963), p. 102.
5 E.g. J. L. Burckhardt, *Travels in Syria and the Holy Land* (London, 1822), p. 609; E. Robinson, *Biblical Researches in Palestine, Mount Sinai and Arabia Petraea* (London, 1841), vol. I, pp. 140–1; Palmer, *The Desert of the Exodus*, pp. 112–18; Lagrange, *RB* 8 (1899), 369–92; A. Alt, *Der Gott der Väter* (Stuttgart, 1929), p. 6 (ET in *Essays*, p. 7); Bright, *History of Israel*, pp. 114–15; Aharoni, *Land of the Bible*, pp. 182–3.
6 R. Lepsius, *A Tour from Thebes to the Peninsula of Sinai* (ET London, 1846), esp. p. 65, and *Briefe aus Aegypten* (Berlin, 1852), pp. 345–54 (letter of 6 April 1845), 447–51; Ebers, *Durch Gosen zum Sinai*, pp. 424ff; C. T. Currelly in W. M. F. Petrie, *Researches in Sinai* (London, 1906), pp. 245–55. *Not* Burckhardt, *pace* J. Baker Greene (*The Hebrew Migration from Egypt*, 2nd edn (London, 1883)) and Harel, *Masʿe Sinai*. For a thorough critique of this view see Schiwietz, *Der Katholik*, 4th series 38 (1908), 9–30, and above, ch. 4 *passim*.
7 C. T. Beke, *Mount Sinai a Volcano* (London, 1873), though Beke abandoned the view that Sinai was a volcano after visiting the Middle East, and opted for a mountain near Akaba, cf. his *Discoveries of Sinai in Arabia* (London, 1878), pp. 400–1; E. Meyer, *Die Israeliten und ihre Nachbarstämme* (Halle, 1906), pp. 67–71; H. Gressmann, *Mose und seine Zeit* (Göttingen, 1913), pp. 409–19; W. J. Phythian-Adams, *PEFQS* 62 (1930), 135–49, 192–209; J. Lewy, *HUCA* 19 (1945–6), 441–2; O. Eissfeldt, *Die Religion in Geschichte und Gegenwart*, 3rd edn (Tübingen, 1957–65), vol. 6, pp. 44–5; J. Koenig, *RHPR* 43 (1963), 2–31, *RHPR* 44 (1964), 200–35; Gese, *Das Ferne und Nahe Wort: Festschrift Leonhard Rost*, *BZAW* 105 (1967), pp. 81–94; von Wissmann, *RE*, supp. vol. 12, cols. 547–51. For a critical review of this theory see B. Zuber, *Vier Studien zu den Ursprüngen Israels*, Orbis Biblicus et Orientalis 9 (Freiburg, 1976), pp. 15–59.
8 Baker Greene, *The Hebrew Migration*, ch. 11; J. Wellhausen, *Prolegomena to the History of Israel* (ET Edinburgh, 1885), p. 344 n. 1 (Gn edn, p. 350 n. 1); A. H. Sayce, *The Early History of the Hebrews* (London, 1897), pp. 186–90; G. B. Gray, *Numbers* (*ICC*) (Edinburgh, 1903), p. 94; Holzinger, *Exodus*, pp. 65–6; Musil, *The Northern Hegaz*, pp. 296–8 (after originally supporting the volcano-theory in his preliminary report, *Im nördlichen Hejaz* (Vienna, 1911)); D. Nielsen, *JPOS* 7 (1927), 187–208; A. Lucas, *The*

Route of the Exodus (London, 1938), pp. 70–9; H. St J. Philby, *The Land of Midian* (London, 1957), pp. 222–3.

9 H. Graetz, *Monatsschrift für Geschichte und Wissenschaft des Judentums* 27 (1878), 337–60; R. Kittel, *Geschichte des Volkes Israel*, 2nd edn (Gotha, 1912), vol. I, pp. 504–11; S. Mowinckel, *Psalmenstudien II* (Oslo, 1922), p. 215 n. 1; T. Wiegand, *Sinai* (Berlin and Leipzig, 1920), pp. 53–4; C. S. Jarvis, *Yesterday and Today in Sinai* (Edinburgh and London, 1936), pp. 141–65; J. P. Hyatt, *Exodus* (London, 1971), p. 206; Herrmann, *History of Israel*, p. 77 (cf. pp. 71–3) (Gn edn, p. 108 (cf. pp. 100–3)).

10 Harel, *Mas'e Sinai*, pp. 274ff. Haran appears from his maps to have adopted this view (*Tequfot uMosadot baMiqra*, pp. 62, 68, 72), but he elsewhere professes ignorance of the location of Sinai (cf. *Tarbiz* 40 (1970–1), 121 n. 11).

11 Baentsch, *Exodus–Numeri*, pp. 138–9; M. Noth, *The History of Israel*, 2nd English edn (London, 1960), pp. 128–32 (1st Gn edn, pp. 110–15).

12 Von Gall, *Altisraelitische Kultstätten*, *BZAW* 3 (1898), pp. 1–22; G. Hölscher, *Festschrift Rudolf Bultmann zum 65. Geburtstag überreicht* (Stuttgart and Cologne, 1949), pp. 127–32; H. H. Rowley, *From Joseph to Joshua* (London, 1950), p. 107 n. 1.

13 Cf. B. Moritz, *Der Sinaikult in heidnischer Zeit* (Berlin, 1916), and the summary in Herrmann, *History of Israel*, p. 72 (Gn edn, p. 101).

14 Cf. de Vaux, *Histoire*, vol. I, p. 402, and in more detail my forthcoming paper, 'The Significance of Dt. 1:2 for the Location of Mount Horeb'.

15 An important collection of passages was published by H. Gunkel, *DLZ* 24 (1903), 3058–9.

16 Cf. Gese, *BZAW* 105 (1967), pp. 91–3, and my critique in *VT* 22 (1972), 152–60.

17 The recent article of von Wissmann (*RE*, supp. vol. 12, cols. 525–52) gives a new consideration of the relevant passages of Ptolemy's *Geography* and advocates the identification of the inland Μαδιάμα with the ruins at Qantara, *c.* 85 km (50 miles) SSW of Tebuk. But he still finds it necessary to reckon with a place called Μαδιάμα at al-Bad' (cols. 544–5), which, contrary to his own assertion (col. 545), could well be the place referred to by Josephus, *AJ* 2.257. But in view of the likelihood of tribal movements, the relevance of Hellenistic/Roman evidence to the location of Biblical Midian must in any case remain doubtful.

18 See W. J. Dumbrell, *VT* 25 (1975), 323–37; also O. Eissfeldt, *JBL* 87 (1968), 383–93, according to whom (cf. p. 385) the Midianites exercised a 'Protektorat' over the whole area later controlled by the Nabataeans (including the Sinai peninsula).

19 Cf. P. J. Parr, G. L. Harding and J. E. Dayton, *Bulletin of the Institute of Archaeology, University of London* 8–9 (1968–9), 238–40; Rothenberg, *Timna*, p. 182.

20 J. R. Bartlett, *JTS* new series 20 (1969), 1–12; de Vaux, *Histoire*, vol. 1, pp. 516–17; Meshel, 'History of the Negev', pp. 106, 148ff.

21 Cf. Bright, *History of Israel*, p. 114: 'Exodus, ch. 19, might equally as well suggest a violent storm.'

22 R. E. Clements, *Exodus* (Cambridge, 1972), p. 114.

23 Cf. J. Jeremias, *Theophanie* (Neukirchen, 1965), pp. 73–90.

24 H. Gressmann, *Die Anfänge Israels* (Göttingen, 1922), p. 64; Alt, *Der Gott der Väter*, p. 6n. (ET *Essays*, p. 7 n. 9); W. F. Albright, *From the Stone Age to Christianity*, 2nd edn (Baltimore, 1957), pp. 262–3; Noth, *History of Israel*, p. 131 (1st Gn edn, p. 114).

25 Cf. D. Baly, *The Geography of the Bible* (London, 1957), p. 222; Zuber, *Vier Studien*, pp. 38–40 (with references to geological literature).

26 So Kittel, *Geschichte des Volkes Israel*, vol. 1, p. 510 n. 2; Zuber, *Vier Studien*, p. 40.

27 *Prolegomena to the History of Israel*, ET pp. 342–3 (Gn edn, pp. 347–9).

28 Surprisingly he did not make any reference to the appearance of the Amalekites in Ex. 17: 8–16, which would be much more intelligible if the episode had occurred at Kadesh, as they are generally associated with the Negeb.

29 See M. Noth, *Überlieferungsgeschichte des Pentateuch* (Stuttgart, 1948), pp. 181–2, for a timely questioning of such views.

30 See n. 10 on p. 108.

31 However Harel's attempt to explain this name on the basis of Arabic *sanna* = 'legislated' and *bašara* = 'brought good tidings' is not convincing. The shape of the mountain (cf. *Masʿe Sinai*, Plate 30) suggests that 'Sin' is more likely to be the Arabic word for 'tooth'. Bisher might be a personal name, as in Robinson, *Biblical Researches*, vol. 1, pp. 52, 61, the name Besharah occurs.

32 This was estimated by C. R. Conder, *PEFQS* 14 (1883), 79, as 'not more than 10 miles [16 km] a day at most'; and by Harel (*Masʿe Sinai*, p. 111) as 'not more than 6 miles [9.6 km] per day'.

33 With M. Noth, *Exodus* (ET London, 1962), p. 32 (Gn edn, p. 20), I regard the addition of 'to Horeb' in 3: 1 as editorial. In my view there is no reason to think that 'Sinai' and 'Horeb' referred to different places, whatever may be the correct explanation of the alternation of the two names: for a recent suggestion see L. Perlitt, in *Beiträge zur Alttestamentlichen Theologie (Festschrift W. Zimmerli)*, ed. H. Donner, R. Hanhart and R. Smend (Göttingen, 1977), pp. 302–22.

34 Cf. Noth, *Überlieferungsgeschichte des Pentateuch*, pp. 150–5; H. Seebass, *Mose und Aaron: Sinai und Gottesberg* (Bonn, 1962), pp. 83–100; R. Smend, *Yahweh War and Tribal Confederacy* (ET Nashville and New York, 1970), pp. 132–4 (Gn edn, pp. 95–6); H. Schmid, *Mose: Überlieferung und Geschichte*, *BZAW* 110 (1968), chs. 3 and 5.

35 *Überlieferungsgeschichte des Pentateuch*, pp. 153–4.

36 This is seen by Noth, ibid. p. 155 n. 400. In any case the objection fails to reckon with the dispersion of the Midianites over a large area (above, pp. 64–5).

37 Cf. N. H. Snaith, *VT* 15 (1965), 395, for examples; also Hölscher, *Festschrift Rudolf Bultmann* (1949), pp. 129–30.

38 Cf. M. Copisarow, *VT* 12 (1962), 5.

39 Cf. Jerome, *Ep.* 78.9.

40 Cf. A. P. Stanley, *Sinai and Palestine* (London, 1858), pp. 5–6 n. 1; Trumbull, *Kadesh–Barnea*, pp. 352ff. Note also Pliny, *Historia Naturalis* 13.25 (quoted by Stanley): 'Rubrum mare et totus orientis oceanus refertus est silvis.'

41 Early on it was vigorously rejected by both Trumbull (see preceding note) and Baker Greene, *The Hebrew Migration*, pp. 68–74.

42 But cf. F. V. Winnett, *The Mosaic Tradition* (Toronto, 1949), p. 86; Simons, *GTTOT*, pp. 77–8; Copisarow, *VT* 12 (1962), 6–13; Snaith, *VT* 15 (1965), 395–8. See also the short note of J. A. Montgomery, *JAOS* 58 (1938), 131–2.

43 For a number of occurrences see Cazelles, *RB* 62 (1955), 341–2. The correspondence of Egyptian *t* to Hebrew ס is quite possible: cf. the examples given by Albright, *The Vocalisation of the Egyptian Syllabic Orthography* (New Haven, 1934), pp. 64–5 (against Simons, *GTTOT*, p. 78). For a detailed discussion of the meaning and relationship of the Hebrew and the Egyptian words see W. A. Ward, *VT* 24 (1974), 339–49 (though he explicitly excludes the expression ים סוף from his discussion (p. 344)).

44 For Yam Suf being the Gulf of Akaba see (e.g.) Ex. 23: 31; Dt. 1: 40; 2: 1; 1 Ki. 9: 26.

45 Cf. Noth, *Festschrift für O. Eissfeldt*, p. 188. Likewise Gressmann, *Mose und seine Zeit*, pp. 415–16, and Schmid, *Mose*, pp. 22–3.

46 Most of the lakes in this area have been favoured by some scholar (cf. the works referred to in n. 1 on p. 107). According to Cazelles an inlet of the Mediterranean Sea is meant, 'the sea *off* Suf' (*RB* 62 (1955), 343).

47 No exact equivalent has yet been found in Egyptian texts; but *pa-twf*, 'the papyrus region', is used for an area in the eastern delta (Cazelles, *RB* 62 (1955), 341–2). Cf. Ward, *VT* 24 (1974), 341–3, who prefers the rendering 'the marshes'.

48 For discussion of the evidence of the itineraries see pp. 80–2.

49 So Snaith, *VT* 15 (1965), 395–8.

50 Cf. the term ים כנרת in the Old Testament, and Jerome, *PL* 23.988 (on Gen. 1: 10).

51 See C. Bourdon, *RB* 41 (1932), 378ff, Simons, *GTTOT*, p. 248, and Haran, *Tequfot uMosadot baMiqra*, pp. 60–1. This theory was very

popular in the second half of the nineteenth century, prior to the almost total acceptance of the Brugsch interpretation of 'Yam Suf'.

52 Albright, *BASOR* 109 (1948), 15; Harel, *Mas'e Sinai*, p. 97.

53 Cf. Bourdon, *RB* 41 (1932), 381 (about 1.5 metres).

54 Glueck, *The Other Side of the Jordan*, p. 107; Rothenberg, *Das Heilige Land* 97 (1965), 27. The age of the 'sill of Shalluf' is not necessarily an obstacle to the theory (cf. Simons, *GTTOT*, p. 248 n. 213).

55 It is sometimes suggested that the second element of the name was not סוּף but סוֹף = 'end' (see Montgomery, *JAOS* 58 (1938), 131–2, Copisarow, *VT* 12 (1962), 12, Ward, *VT* 24 (1974), 344 – cf. LXX at 3 Kms. (= 1 Ki.) 9: 26 τῆς ἐσχάτης θαλάσσης). But the occurrences of סוֹף in the Old Testament appear all to be post-exilic (and influenced by Aramaic?), which makes its appearance in an ancient Hebrew toponym rather improbable (cf. de Vaux, *Histoire*, vol. 1, p. 355). סוּף in Dt. 1: 1 may be related in some way, but is itself in need of elucidation.

56 Palmer, *The Desert of the Exodus*, pp. 349–58, 509–15; Trumbull, *Kadesh–Barnea*. The modern dissentients are relatively few: Musil, *The Northern Hegaz*, pp. 262–6; Hommel, *Ethnologie und Geographie*, pp. 621, 629–31; W. J. Phythian-Adams, *The Call of Israel* (Oxford, 1934), pp. 195–200; Winnett, *The Mosaic Tradition*, pp. 95–105; G. Hort, *Australian Biblical Review* 7 (1959), 2–26; H. Bar-Deroma, *PEQ* 96 (1964), 101–34.

57 For a survey of earlier views see Trumbull, *Kadesh–Barnea*, pp. 185–234.

58 For a full discussion of all the passages see Trumbull, *Kadesh–Barnea*. Aharoni considers Ain el Qudeirat, about 5 miles (8 km) NNW of Ain Qadeis, to be a more likely site (in Rothenberg and Aharoni, *God's Wilderness*, p. 122). The transference of an ancient name to an adjacent feature is not uncommon (Aharoni, *Land of the Bible*, pp. 112–13). See also C. H. J. de Geus, *Oudtestamentische Studien* 20 (1977), 56–66.

59 This is implied by the passages which make the southern border of Judah contiguous with Edom (Num. 34: 3; Jos. 15: 1, 21).

Notes to Chapter 8

1 See the maps of Aharoni, *Land of the Bible*, p. 180, and Haran, *Tequfot uMosadot baMiqra*, p, 50.

2 So Haran, *Tequfot uMosadot baMiqra*, p. 49.

3 Our main sources of information have been: Robinson, *Biblical Researches*, vol. 1, pp. 104–7, 291–3, 561–5 (Note XXII); Harel, *Mas'e Sinai*, pp. 49–53; Rothenberg, *PEQ* 102 (1970), 4–29; Haran, *Tequfot uMosadot baMiqra*, pp. 49–55. I have been unable to make use of A. Ammar, 'Ancient and Modern Routes in Sinai', *Bulletin de la Société Royale de Géographie d'Égypte* 21 (1946), 371–492 (in Arabic: cited by Harel).

4 Cf. A. H. Gardiner, *JEA* 6 (1920), 99–116; *Tabula Peutingeriana*; *Itinerarium Antonini* (ed. Cuntz, pp. 21, 23).

5 On this route see T. E. Lawrence and C. L. Woolley, *The Wilderness of Zin*, PEF Annual 3, 1914–15 (London, 1915), pp. 39ff.

6 Contrast J. A. Wilson, *JNES* 14 (1955), 228 ('only by Bedouin') with N. Glueck, *BASOR* 71 (1938), 7. The view that this route is the one marked between Clysma and Aila on the *Tabula Peutingeriana* is perhaps in need of revision (see above, p. 48).

7 Smith, *Historical Geography*, p. 134. Recent archaeological discoveries at Kuntilat Ajrud (an eighth-century BC building and numerous inscriptions) indicate the antiquity of this route (cf. Z. Meshel, *BA* 39 (1976), 6–10, and *Qadmoniot* 9 (1976), 119–24).

8 Y. Aharoni, *IEJ* 4 (1954), 9–16, suggested a route passing through the southern Negeb highlands further to the north-east. But this is not an easy route, and the earlier suggestion of P. Thomsen (*ZDPV* 29 (1906), 101) that the southern part of Darb el-Ġazza is referred to both on the *Tabula* and in Ptolemy's list of settlements in Arabia Petraea (*Geography* 5.17) should probably be retained (so Z. Meshel and Y. Tsafrir, *PEQ* 107 (1975), 20). It remains possible that the ancient route entered Wadi Arabah some distance north of Eilat, perhaps by the route through Wadi Beyarah noted by Robinson, *Biblical Researches*, vol. 1, pp. 268, 292.

9 On the name see Haran, *Tequfot uMosadot baMiqra*, pp. 54–5.

10 Cf. Albright, *BASOR* 109 (1948), 5–20.

11 *PEQ* 102 (1970), 18–21. See also Negev, *Inscriptions*. The pilgrim-route from the Sinai monastery is mentioned by both Theodosius (*De Situ Terrae Sanctae* 27) and Anonymus Placentinus (*Itin.* 40).

12 *Biblical Researches*, vol. 1, pp. 291–3, 561–5.

13 Robinson (pp. 293, 563) was of the opinion that this was the route used by Christian pilgrims of the fifteenth and sixteenth centuries.

Notes to Chapter 9

1 My literary analysis (cf. n. 3 on p. 107) assigns the following itinerary-notes to P: Ex. 19: 1; Num. 10: 12; 20: 1aα; 22: 1.

2 E. L. Uphill has discussed the suggestions that have been made and argued a convincing case for Qantir (*JNES* 27 (1968), 299–316, *JNES* 28 (1969), 15–39); cf. Bietak, *Tell el Daba II*.

3 Cf. Cazelles, *RB* 62 (1955), 354–7; W. Helck, *VT* 15 (1965), 35–40, who defends the identification with Tell el Maskhuta despite the absence of the city-determinative. Pithom is located by Uphill (*JNES* 27 (1968), 292–9) at On/Heliopolis, but his arguments are not persuasive.

4 Here too there is no problem over the correspondence of *t* to Hebrew כ (*pace* Simons, *GTTOT*, p. 247 n. 210), but the interpretation of Succoth as a genuine Semitic name remains a possibility. It was the view favoured by H. Brugsch (*L'Exode et les monuments égyptiens* (Leipzig, 1875),

pp. 12–13), and is maintained in a slightly different form by Simons, *GTTOT*, pp. 246–7.

5 Simons, *GTTOT*, p. 247; cf. *ANET*, p. 259.

6 Cf. Cazelles, *RB* 62 (1955), 358–60. But surely Sile would have been referred to by its usual name, and not by a mere appellative?

7 So Brugsch, *L'Exode*; O. Eissfeldt, *Baal-zaphon, Zeus Casios und der Durchzug der Israeliten durchs Meer* (Halle, 1932), pp. 48–65; Noth, *Festschrift für O. Eissfeldt*, pp. 184–5; Cazelles, *RB* 62 (1955), 321–54; Aharoni, *Land of the Bible*, p. 179; Dothan, *Proceedings of the Fifth World Congress of Jewish Studies, 1969*, 223–4; G. Fohrer, *History of Israelite Religion* (ET London, 1973), p. 72 (Gn edn, p. 59); S. Herrmann, *Israel in Egypt* (ET London, 1973), pp. 60ff (Gn edn, pp. 87–91); S. Norin, *Er Spaltete das Meer* (Lund, 1977), pp. 32–3.

8 Cf. A. H. Gardiner, *Recueil Champollion*, Bibliothèque de l'École des Hautes Études, Sci. Hist. et Phil., 234 (Paris, 1922), pp. 203–15; Aly Bei Shafei, *Bulletin de la Société Royale de Géographie d'Égypte* 21 (1946), 231–87; W. F. Albright, *Festschrift A. Bertholet*, ed. W. Baumgartner *et al.* (Tübingen, 1950), pp. 1–14; G. E. Wright, *Biblical Archaeology* (London, 1962), pp. 60–2; Bright, *History of Israel*, p. 112.

9 Serapeum, south of Lake Timsah, was popular around the turn of the century, due to the influence of E. Naville (e.g. *The Route of the Exodus* (London, 1891)) and Lagrange (*RB* 9 (1900), 74–80). Since the work of Clédat a more southerly point has been preferred: cf. Bourdon, *RB* 41 (1932), 538–49, followed by Abel, *Géographie*, vol. 2, pp. 208–10, Simons, *GTTOT*, pp. 248–51, and Harel, *Mas'e Sinai*, pp. 225–31. See also W. Helck, *TLZ* 97 (1972), 182, though it is not clear whether he thinks that these names themselves point to this region. Haran, *Tequfot uMosadot baMiqra*, pp. 58–61, holds that the itinerary (his 'P') refers to the Lake Timsah region, but E (and J?) to the Bitter Lakes.

10 See however the article of Servin, *BIE* 31 (1948–9), 315–55, which significantly takes for granted that the tradition reported by Etheria is accurate.

11 See above, n. 50 on p. 112.

12 Cazelles, *RB* 62 (1955), 321–54.

13 Possibly two adjacent sites are involved: cf. E. Oren, *Qadmoniot* 10 (1977), 71–6. For Migdol (Magdolum) in the *It. Ant.* see Cuntz *Itineraria*, vol. 1, p. 23.

14 For the text see *ANET*, p. 259. It is of particular interest because, in addition to the Migdol, it also mentions *Tkw* and a *ḥtm*, in the same order as in the itineraries.

15 Cf. G. Daressy, *Sphinx* 14 (1910–11), 155–71, especially 169–70. Places near the Mediterranean coast appear separately in 2.14–17.

16 Cf. Eissfeldt, *Baal-zaphon*, pp. 1–7; A. Goetze, *BASOR* 79 (1940), 33.

But the Egyptian Mount Casios must be located, in view of ancient geographical texts cited by Cazelles (*RB* 62 (1955), 333–5), not at Mahammadiye (Eissfeldt) but at Ras Qasrun on the spit separating Lake Sirbonis from the sea, where recent Israeli exploration has brought to light a variety of remains from the Iron Age and later: cf. M. Dothan, *IEJ* 17 (1967), 279–80; *IEJ* 18 (1968), 255–6, and more fully in *Eretz Israel* 9 (1969), 47–59.

17 The earliest clear references are Herodotus, *History* 2.6, 158, 3.5. So far the Israeli exploration (see preceding note) seems to have produced no cultic objects older than the Hellenistic period, although the occupation of the site certainly began before then. In fact the only possibly cultic objects reported so far are some inscribed fragments of stone, whose cultic connections are not at all clear. Cazelles (*RB* 62 (1955), 335–6) has noted the occurrence of *ḥtyn* in a section of Papyrus Anastasi I (27.4) relating to the Mediterranean coast (*ANET*, p. 478: Husayin). He would like to see this as an early reference to the place by the use of an equivalent to the name Casios: this is at any rate a possibility.

18 For the cult at Tahpanhes/Daphnae see *KAI* 50.2–3 (sixth century BC), which led Albright to locate Baal-zephon there (*Festschrift A. Bertholet*, pp. 1–14); at a much earlier period the god was among those worshipped at Memphis (Sallier papyrus IV Rs. 1.6: *ANET*, pp. 249–50 (cf. the *addendum* on p. 673 of the 3rd edn)); and in the Ptolemaic period a Migdol was named after him (see above). On the wide popularity of the Baal-zaphon/Zeus Casios cult in the Mediterranean lands as far west as Marseilles see H. Gese, M. Höfner and K. Rudolph, *Die Religionen Altsyriens, Altarabiens und der Mandäer* (Stuttgart, 1970), pp. 125ff.

19 This difficulty, half-recognised by Cazelles (*RB* 62 (1955), 362), is avoided by Dothan's view, that Migdol might be 'one of the tells east of the lake' (sc. Sirbonis) (*IEJ* 17 (1967), 280).

20 Although it would be a methodological error to assume that the Old Testament presents a single view of the route, it is relevant to note that no other evidence requires a northerly location for 'the sea', and some is positively against it (Ex. 13: 17–18). Possibly the reference to Baal-zephon is not an original part of the itinerary: in which case its location need not be decisive for the identification of the basic route (so Winnett, *The Mosaic Tradition*, p. 84; and see my dissertation, 'The Wilderness Itineraries', pp. 86–7).

21 On Ezion-Geber see pp. 85–6. The equation of Elim with Eloth/Elath was advocated by (e.g.) Baker Greene, *The Hebrew Migration*, pp. 170–2, Gressmann, *Mose und seine Zeit*, p. 414 n. 12, Hommel, *Ethnologie und Geographie*, pp. 625–8, and J. Koenig, *RHR* 166 (1964), 137.

22 Such an interpretation could find additional support in the arguments put forward by G. W. Coats, *VT* 17 (1967), 253–65.

23 The location of Elim at et-Tur (Meyer, *Die Israeliten und ihre Nachbar-stämme*, pp. 100ff, Phythian-Adams, *The Call of Israel*, p. 126 n. 1, Schmid, *Mose*, p. 18 n. 4), in conformity with one branch of early Christian tradition (see above, p. 38), can perhaps find some support in a passage of the Greek geographer Agatharchides (*apud* Diodorus Siculus 3.42.2–4, 43.1, and Strabo, *Geography* 16.4.18) which mentions a place called Phoenicon, located in this general area, with a sacred grove (cf. Ex. 15:27?). But the details of the text are not clear, and it is also possible that this Phoenicon was on the Gulf of Akaba (Hommel, *Ethnologie und Geographie*, pp. 625–6) or closer to the head of the Gulf of Suez, where Cosmas seems to have known a place of this name (see above, p. 43). In any case, the distance of et-Tur from the presumed place of the 'sea-crossing' hardly permits its identification with Elim.

24 The former identification appears already in Burckhardt, *Travels in Syria and the Holy Land*, pp. 472–3, the latter in Robinson, *Biblical Researches*, vol. 1, p. 105.

25 For these suggestions see Simons, *GTTOT*, pp. 252–3 and, in more detail, Abel, *Géographie*, vol. 2, p. 213.

26 Robinson, *Biblical Researches*, vol. 1, pp. 131–2, 138–41.

27 *Travels in Syria and the Holy Land*, p. 495.

28 Arabic *ḍ* regularly appears in Hebrew cognates or equivalents as צ, which is represented by 'z' in the normal English transcription of 'Hazeroth': e.g. Heb. אָרֶץ, Ar. *arḍun* = 'land'.

29 Cf. *BDB*, pp. 347–8.

30 For the once popular identification of Ezion-Geber with Ain Ġadyan cf. Smith, *Historical Geography*, p. 368 (with further references). On the name itself see Koehler, *ZDPV* 59 (1936), 193–5.

31 F. Frank, *ZDPV* 57 (1934), 244; Glueck, *The Other Side of the Jordan*, pp. 106–37; Meshel, 'History of the Negev', ch. F, especially pp. 134–8.

32 This might of course explain the shipwreck of 1 Ki. 22: 48.

33 Cf. Robinson, *Biblical Researches*, vol. 1, p. 251n.

34 Cf. *Das Heilige Land* 97 (1965), 18–28; *PEQ* 102 (1970), 4; *Timna*, pp. 202–7. In 1961 Aharoni, holding to Glueck's identification of Ezion-Geber, proposed locating Jotbathah and early Christian Jotabe at Jezirat Faraun (in Rothenberg and Aharoni, *God's Wilderness*, pp. 163–4). But at least as far as Jotbathah is concerned this suggestion is less likely than the older view that it was at Ain Ġadyan (see pp. 92–3).

35 Cf. Bartlett, *JTS* new series 20 (1969), 1–12.

36 The possible location of Jotbathah at Ain Ġadyan (see pp. 92–3) would point to this interpretation of MT. In the nineteenth century those who wished to harmonise the conceptions of the route which I would attribute to D and P (see my dissertation, 'The Wilderness Itineraries', pp. 110–13) found in the MT order of the names evidence that Israel was at (or

near) Kadesh twice (e.g. Robinson, *Biblical Researches*, vol. 2, pp. 609ff, Trumbull, *Kadesh–Barnea*, pp. 147ff).

37 So Palmer, *Desert of the Exodus*, pp. 508–9

38 J. Koenig, *Le site de al-Jaw dans l'ancien pays de Madian* (Paris, 1971).

39 Ibid. pp. 209–36.

40 J. Pirenne, *RB* 82 (1975), 35–69.

41 Cf. also Zuber, *Vier Studien*, 40–9.

42 Noth, *PJB* 36 (1940), 5–28.

43 Gese, *BZAW* 105 (1967), pp. 85ff.

44 de Vaux, *Histoire*, vol. 1, pp. 405, 407, 519.

45 Zuber, *Vier Studien*, 61–72.

46 Koenig, *RHR* 166 (1964), 121–41.

47 Musil, *The Northern Hegaz*, 188ff.

48 T. E. Lawrence, *Seven Pillars of Wisdom* (1939 edn), vol. 1, pp. 245–7.

49 On the question of the Roman route see above, n. 8 on p. 114.

50 Ed. Seeck, p. 74.43. Cf. Abel, *Géographie*, vol. 2, p. 182, and de Vaux, *Histoire*, vol. 1, p. 520.

51 Curiously Aharoni reproduced this widespread error in his text (*Land of the Bible*, p. 185), while at the same time making a much more plausible (if still not ideal) suggestion in his 'List of Site Identifications' (p. 385), where Zalmonah is tentatively identified with es-Salmaneh, the name of a wadi which descends from the high ground east of Wadi Arabah between Khirbet Feinan and the Dead Sea (cf. Palmer, *Desert of the Exodus*, p. 458).

52 *PJB* 36 (1940), 10–17, modified in his *Josua*, 2nd edn (Tübingen, 1953), pp. 29, 81. On Almon-Diblathaim see also H. Cazelles, *VT* 9 (1959), 413–15. In addition to those referred to in the text, Noth proposed the following identifications: Almon-Diblathaim – near Khirbet et-Têm; the mountain of Abarim, before Nebo – in the vicinity of Mount Nebo on the heights overlooking the Dead Sea on the east; Beth-Jeshimoth – Tell el-ʿAẓēme; Abel-Shittim – Tell el-Hammam. For fuller details of the locations of the modern sites see his discussion.

53 Wadi el-Weibeh, about 10 miles [16 km] north of Khirbet Feinan, is the most probable site (Lagrange, *RB* 9 (1900), 286), but it is rather close to the site of Punon/Pinon. AinʿUbur (L. Vestri, *Bibbia e Oriente* 6 (1964), 86–93) is too far east, and has an additional consonant as well as the wrong guttural. Khirbet Ǵuweibe (mentioned by Noth, *PJB* 36 (1940), 17 n. 1) has the wrong guttural as well as being rather too close to Khirbet Feinan (10 km, according to Noth).

54 *Land of the Bible*, pp. 51–2. The importance of this route is also asserted by de Vaux, *Histoire*, vol. 1, p. 520, and Haran, *Tequfot uMosadot baMiqra*, p. 73.

55 Cf. Robinson, *Biblical Researches*, vol. 2, p. 610; Stanley, *Sinai and Palestine*, pp. 86n., 94.

56 Cf. Trumbull, *Kadesh–Barnea*, pp. 132ff; Lagrange, *RB* 9 (1900), 280; Aharoni, in Rothenberg and Aharoni, *God's Wilderness*, pp. 137ff; N. Glueck, *Rivers in the Desert*, revised edn (New York, 1968), p. 206.

57 Cf. Palmer, *Desert of the Exodus*, pp. 523–5; Simons, *GTTOT*, p. 261.

58 Little seems to be known about routes in Moab apart from the great north–south routes: cf. A. H. van Zyl, *The Moabites* (Leiden, 1960), pp. 60–1.

59 Palmer, *Desert of the Exodus*, p. 525.

60 Cf. Smith, *Historical Geography*, p. 380; Gray, *Numbers*, pp. 291–2.

61 Cf. *KAI* 181.27. For the omission of the element 'Beth-' in a name see Aharoni, *Land of the Bible*, p. 97.

62 On the textual problem see n. 36 on p. 101; on the question of the unity of the verse cf. O. Eissfeldt, *Hexateuchsynopse* (Leipzig, 1922), pp. 63–4. The location of Pisgah east of the north end of the Dead Sea is clear enough from other passages (Dt. 3: 17, 27; 34: 1). But taken by itself 'the valley' (if that is the correct reading) would not provide such a clear end-point for this itinerary.

63 What could be the ancient site has been excavated by Meshel; see *IEJ* 24 (1974), 273–4.

BIBLIOGRAPHY
AND AUTHOR INDEX

Bold figures indicate the place or places in this volume where the work is referred to.

Abel, F.-M., *Géographie de la Palestine*, Études Bibliques (Paris, 1933, 1938) **98 n. 29, 99 n. 4, n. 5, 102 n. 39, 115 n. 9, 117 n. 25, 118 n. 50**

Aharoni, Y., 'The Roman Road to Aila/Eilat', *IEJ* 4 (1954), 9–16 **90, 114 n. 8**

The Land of the Bible (London, 1966) **62, 90, 99 n. 33, 108 n. 14, 109 n. 1, n. 5, 113 n. 58, n. 1, 115 n. 7, 118 n. 51, n. 54, 119 n. 61**

Aharoni, Y., and Avi-Yonah, M., *The Macmillan Bible Atlas* (London and New York, 1968) **98 n. 32**

Albright, W. F., *The Vocalisation of the Egyptian Syllabic Orthography* (New Haven, 1934) **112 n. 43**

'Exploring in Sinai with the University of California African Expedition', *BASOR* 109 (1948), 5–20 **113 n. 52, 114 n. 10**

'Baalzephon', *Festschrift A. Bertholet*, ed. W. Baumgartner *et al.* (Tübingen, 1950), 1–14 **80, 115 n. 8, 116 n. 18**

From the Stone Age to Christianity (Baltimore, 1957) **111 n. 24**

Alexander, P. S., 'The Toponymy of the Targumim', unpublished D.Phil. thesis, University of Oxford, 1974 **17, 94 n. 4 (ch. 1), 96 n. 19, n. 2, 97 n. 11**

Alt, A., *Der Gott der Väter* (Stuttgart, 1929), ET in *Essays on Old Testament History and Religion* (Oxford, 1966), pp. 1–77 **109 n. 5, 111 n. 24**

Altaner, B., and Stuiber, A., *Patrologie* (Freiburg, 1966) **99 n. 3, 104 n. 75, n. 76, 105 n. 85**

Ammar, A., 'Ancient and Modern Routes in Sinai', *Bulletin de la Société Royale de Géographie d'Égypte* 21 (1946), 371–492 (Arabic) **113 n. 3**

Avi-Yonah, M., *The Madeba Mosaic Map* (Jerusalem, 1954) **105 n. 92, n. 93**

Gazeteer of Roman Palestine, Qedem Monographs, vol. 5 (Jerusalem, 1976) **96 n. 20, 97 n. 14, 101 n. 29, n. 35, n. 37, 102 n. 39**

Baentsch, B., *Exodus–Numeri* (Göttingen, 1903) **107 n. 1, 110 n. 11**

Baly, D., *The Geography of the Bible* (London, 1957) **111 n. 25**

Geographical Companion to the Bible (London, 1963) **109 n. 4**

Bar-Deroma, H., 'Kadesh–Barnea', *PEQ* 96 (1964), 101–34 **113 n. 56**

Barthélemy, D., *Les devanciers d'Aquila*, *SVT* 10 (Leiden, 1963) **95 n. 13**

Bartlett, J. R., 'The Land of Seir and the Brotherhood of Edom', *JTS* new series 20 (1969), 1–20 **111 n. 20, 117 n. 35**

Bauer, J. B., 'Drei Tage', *Biblica* 39 (1958), 354–8 **108 n. 8**

Beck, E., *Des heiligen Ephraem des Syrers Hymnen auf Abraham Kidunaya und Julianos Saba, CSCO*, Scriptores Syri, vols. 140-1 (Louvain, 1972) **101 n. 23**

Beke, C. T., *Mount Sinai a Volcano* (London, 1873) **109 n. 7**
Discoveries of Sinai in Arabia (London, 1878) **109 n. 7**

Bietak, M., *Tell el Daba II* (Vienna, 1975) **96 n. 23, 114 n. 2**

Boraas, R., Geraty, L. T., *et al.*, 'Heshbon 1974', *AUSS* 14 (1976), 1–216 **102 n. 39**

Boraas, R., Horn, S. H., *et al.*, 'Heshbon 1968', *AUSS* 7 (1969), 97–239 **102 n. 39**
'Heshbon 1971', *AUSS* 11 (1973), 1–144 **102 n. 39**
'Heshbon 1973', *AUSS* 13 (1975), 101–247 **102 n. 39**

Bourdon, C., 'La route de l'Exode', *RB* 41 (1932), 370–92, 538–49 **112 n. 51, 113 n. 53, 115 n. 9**

Bowker, J. W., *The Targums and Rabbinic Judaism* (Cambridge, 1969) **94 n. 1 (ch. 2), 97 n. 7, 98 n. 20**

Bright J., *History of Israel* (London, 1960) **96 n. 23, 109 n. 5, 111 n. 21, 115 n. 8**

Brown, F., Driver, S. R. and Briggs, C. A., *A Hebrew and English Lexicon of the Old Testament*, reprinted with corrections (Oxford, 1953) **98 n. 17, 117 n. 29**

Brugsch, H., *L'Exode et les monuments égyptiens* (Leipzig, 1875) **70, 71, 113 n. 51, 114 n. 4, 115 n. 7**

Burckhardt, J. L., *Travels in Syria and the Holy Land* (London, 1822) **85, 109 n. 5, n. 6, 117 n. 24, n. 27**

Cazelles, H., 'Les localisations de l'Exode et la critique littéraire', *RB* 62 (1955), 321–54 **81, 82, 107 n. 1, 112 n. 43, n. 46, n. 47, 114 n. 3, 115 n. 6, n. 7, n. 12, 116 n. 16, n. 17, n. 18**
'Tophel (Dt. 1.1)', *VT* 9 (1959), 412–15 **118 n. 52**

Chitty, D. J., *The Desert a City* (Oxford, 1966) **100 n. 23, 102 n. 47, 103 n. 50**

Clements, R. E., *Exodus* (Cambridge, 1972) **111 n. 22**

Coats, G. W., 'The Traditio-historical Character of the Reed Sea Motif', *VT* 17 (1967), 253–65 **116 n. 22**
'The Wilderness Itinerary', *CBQ* 34 (1972), 135–52 **94 n. 1 (ch. 1)**

Conder, C. R., 'The Exodus', *PEFQS* 14 (1883), 79–90 **111 n. 32**

Copisarow, M., 'The Ancient Egyptian, Greek and Hebrew Concept of the Red Sea', *VT* 12 (1962), 1–13 **112 n. 38, n. 42, 113 n. 55**

Cross, F. M., 'The History of the Biblical Text in the Light of Discoveries in the Judaean Desert', *HTR* 57 (1964), 281–99 **95 n. 13**

Daressy, G., 'La liste géographique du papyrus no. 31169 du Caire', *Sphinx* 14 (1910–11), 155–71 **115 n. 15**

Davies, G. I., 'Hagar, el Heğra and the Location of Mount Sinai (with an

Additional Note on Reqem) ', *VT* 22 (1972), 152–63 **17, 64, 97 n. 8, n. 10, n. 12, 99 n. 2, n. 7, 110 n. 16**

'A Fragment of an Early Recension of the Greek Exodus ', *IOSCS Bulletin* 7 (1974), 22–3 (summary of paper read at the Oxford Biblical Congress 1973) **95 n. 14**

'The Wilderness Itineraries: a Comparative Study ', *TB* 25 (1974), 46–81 **94 n. 1 (ch. 1), 108 n. 5**

'The Wilderness Itineraries in the Old Testament ', unpublished Ph.D. dissertation, University of Cambridge, 1975 **107 n. 3, 116 n. 20**

'The Significance of Dt. 1 : 2 for the Location of Mount Horeb ', forthcoming in *PEQ* **98 n. 23, 110 n. 14**

Devréesse, R., 'Le christianisme dans la péninsule sinaïtique ', *RB* 49 (1940), 205–23 **100 n. 23, 102 n. 47, 103 n. 50**

Diez Macho, A., 'The Recently Discovered Palestinian Targum: Its Antiquity and Relationship with the other Targums ', *SVT* 7 (1960), 222–45 **96 n. 2**

Dillmann, A., *Die Bücher Numeri, Deuteronomium und Josua*, 2nd edn (Leipzig, 1886) **107 n. 1**

Donner, H., and Cüppers, H., 'Die Restauration und Konservierung der Mosaikkarte von Madeba ', *ZDPV* 83 (1967), 1–33 **105 n. 92, n. 94**

Dothan, M., 'Notes and News: Lake Sirbonis (Sabkhat el-Bardawil) ', *IEJ* 17 (1967), 279–80 and 18 (1968), 255–6 **116 n. 16, n. 19**

'An Archaeological Survey of Mount Casius and Vicinity ', *Eretz Israel* 9 (1969), 47–59 (Heb.) **116 n. 16**

'The Exodus in the Light of an Archaeological Survey in (*sic*) Lake Sirbonis ', *Proceedings of the Fifth World Congress of Jewish Studies, 1969*, 223–4 **115 n. 7**

Dumbrell, W. J., 'Midian – a Land or a League? ', *VT* 25 (1975), 323–37 **110 n. 18**

Ebers, G., *Durch Gosen zum Sinai*, 2nd edn (Leipzig, 1881) **95 n. 17, 100 n. 22, 104 n. 78, 109 n. 6**

Eissfeldt, O., *Hexateuchsynopse* (Leipzig, 1922: repr. Darmstadt, 1962) **119 n. 62**

Baal-zaphon, Zeus Casios und der Durchzug der Israeliten durchs Meer (Halle, 1932) **115 n. 7, n. 16, 116 n. 16**

'Sinai ', in *Die Religion in Geschichte und Gegenwart*, 3rd edn (Tübingen, 1957–65), vol. 6, cols. 44–5 **109 n. 7**

'Protektorat der Midianiter über ihre Nachbarn im letzten Viertel des 2. Jahrtausend v. Chr.', *JBL* 87 (1968), 383–93 **110 n. 18**

Encyclopaedia Judaica (Jerusalem, 1971) **97 n. 14**

Encyclopaedia Miqraith (Jerusalem, 1964–) **98 n. 27**

Éthérie, Journal de voyage, ed. H. Pétré, Sources Chrétiennes 21 (Paris, 1948) **41, 103 n. 54, n. 63, n. 70, 104 n. 71**

Ewald, H., *Geschichte des Volkes Israel*, 3rd edn (Göttingen, 1864–8) **60, 67, 85, 108 n. 10**

Fohrer, G., *History of Israelite Religion* (ET London, 1973), Gn edn *Geschichte der israelitischen Religion* (Berlin, 1969) **115 n. 7**

Frank, F., 'Aus der Arabah', *ZDPV* 57 (1934), 208–78 **85, 117 n. 31**

Gager, J. G., *Moses in Greco-Roman Paganism*, Society of Biblical Literature Monographs, vol. 16 (Nashville and New York, 1972) **96 n. 22, 99 n. 7**

von Gall, A., *Altisraelitische Kultstätten*, *BZAW* 3 (Giessen, 1898) **49, 55, 106 n. 1, n. 13, 110 n. 12**

Gardiner, A. H., 'The Ancient Military Road Between Egypt and Palestine', *JEA* 6 (1920), 99–116 **113 n. 4**

'The Geography of the Exodus', *Recueil Champollion*, Bibliothèque de l'École des Hautes Études, Sci. Hist. et Phil. 234 (Paris, 1922), 203–15 **115 n. 8**

Gese, H., 'τὸ δὲ "Αγαρ Σινᾶ ὄρος ἐστὶν ἐν τῇ 'Αραβίᾳ', in *Das Ferne und Nahe Wort: Festschrift Leonhard Rost*, *BZAW* 105 (Berlin, 1967), 81–94 **64, 88, 95 n. 16, 99 n. 2, 109 n. 9, 110 n. 16, 118 n. 43**

Gese, H., Höfner, M. and Rudolph, K., *Die Religionen Altsyriens, Altarabiens und der Mandäer* (Stuttgart, 1970) **116 n. 18**

de Geus, C. H. J., 'Kadesh-Barnea: some geographical and historical remarks', *Oudtestamentische Studien*, 20 (1977), 56–66 **113 n. 58**

Giveon, R., *Les bédouins shosou des documents égyptiens* (Leiden, 1971) **108 n. 4**

Glueck, N., 'The First Campaign at Tell el-Kheleifeh (Ezion-Geber)', *BASOR* 71 (1938), 3–17 **85, 114 n. 6**

Rivers in the Desert, revised edn (New York, 1968) **119 n. 56**

The Other Side of the Jordan, revised edn (Cambridge, Mass., 1970) **74, 85, 108 n. 11, 113 n. 54, 117 n. 31, n. 34**

Goetze, A., 'The City Khalbi and the Khapiru people', *BASOR* 79 (1940), 32–4 **115 n. 16**

Gold, V. R., 'The Mosaic Map of Madeba', *BA* 21 (1958), 50–71 **105 n. 92**

Graetz, H., 'Die Lage des Sinai oder Horeb', *Monatsschrift für Geschichte und Wissenschaft des Judentums* 27 (1878), 337–60 **110 n. 9**

Gray, G. B., *Numbers (ICC)* (Edinburgh, 1903) **109 n. 8, 119 n. 60**

Greene, J. Baker, *The Hebrew Migration from Egypt*, 2nd edn (London, 1883) **109 n. 6, n. 8, 112 n. 41, 116 n. 21**

Gressmann, H., *Mose und seine Zeit* (Göttingen, 1913) **109 n. 7, 112 n. 45, 116 n. 21**

Die Anfänge Israels (Göttingen, 1922) **111 n. 24**

Gunkel, H., 'Notiz', *DLZ* 24 (1903), 3058–9 **110 n. 15**

Haran, M., 'Darkehem shel Yotze Mitzraim', *Tarbiz* 40 (1970–1), 113–43 (substantially the same as *Tequfot* (see next entry), 37–76) **110 n. 10**

Tequfot uMosadot baMiqra (Tel Aviv, 1972) **107 n. 2, 110 n. 2, 112 n. 51, 113 n. 1, n. 2, n. 3, 114 n. 9, 115 n. 9, 118 n. 54**

Harel, M., 'Sinai', in *Encyclopaedia Miqraith*, vol. 5, cols. 1021–2 **98 n. 27**

Mas'e Sinai (Tel Aviv, 1968) (in large measure drawn from the author's dissertation 'The Route of the Exodus of the Israelites from Egypt', submitted to New York University (in English) in 1964) **37–8, 103 n. 52, 104 n. 78, 106 n. 3, 107 n. 1, 109 n. 6, 110 n. 10, 111 n. 31, n. 32, 112 n. 52, 113 n. 3, 115 n. 9**

Hatch, E. and Redpath, H. A., *A Concordance to the Septuagint* (Oxford, 1897; Supplement 1900, 1906) **95 n. 5**

Helck, W., '*Tkw* und die Ramses-Stadt', *VT* 15 (1965), 35–48 **114 n. 3**

Review of S. Herrmann, *Israels Aufenthalt in Ägypten*, *TLZ* 97 (1972), 178–82 **115 n. 9**

Henninger, J., 'Nil le Sinaïtique', *DBS* 6.475–80 **102 n. 47**

Herrmann, S., *Israel in Egypt* (ET London, 1973), Gn edn *Israels Aufenthalt in Ägypten* (Stuttgart, 1970) **115 n. 7**

A History of Israel (ET London, 1975), Gn edn *Geschichte Israels in alttestamentlicher Zeit* (Munich, 1973) **108 n. 4, 110 n. 9, n. 13**

Hölscher, G., 'Sinai und Choreb', *Festschrift Rudolf Bultmann zum 65. Geburtstag überreicht* (Stuttgart and Köln, 1949), pp. 127–32 **110 n. 12, 112 n. 37**

Holzinger, H., *Exodus* (Tübingen, 1900) **95 n. 17, 109 n. 8**

Hommel, F., *Ethnologie und Geographie des Alten Orients*, Handbuch der Altertumswissenschaft III/1/1 (Munich, 1926) **97 n. 10, 113 n. 56, 116 n. 21, 117 n. 23**

Hort, G., 'Musil, Madian and the Mountain of the Law', *Jewish Studies for G. Sicher* (Prague, 1955), 81–93 **106 n. 2, 107 n. 18**

'The Death of Korah', *Australian Biblical Review* 7 (1959), 2–26 **113 n. 56**

Hyatt, J. P., *Exodus* (London, 1971) **110 n. 9**

Illustrium Christi Martyrum Lecti Triumphi, ed. F. Combefis (Paris, 1660) **103 n. 49, n. 53**

Isenberg, S. R., 'On the Jewish–Palestinian Origins of the Peshitta to the Pentateuch', *JBL* 90 (1971), 69–81 **97 n. 6**

Itinera Hierosolymitana, Corpus Scriptorum Ecclesiasticorum Latinorum, vol. 39, ed. P. Geyer (repr. New York and London, 1964) **103 n. 54, n. 56, 104 n. 75, 105 n. 84**

Itineraria Romana, ed. O. Cuntz, vol. 1 (Leipzig, 1929) **105 n. 86, 113 n. 4, 115 n. 13**

Jarvis, C. S., *Yesterday and Today in Sinai* (Edinburgh and London, 1936) **110 n. 9**

Jeremias, J., *Theophanie* (Neukirchen, 1965) **111 n. 23**

The Jewish Encyclopedia (New York and London, 1906) **96 n. 4**

Jones, A. H. M., *The Cities of the Eastern Roman Provinces*, 2nd edn (Oxford, 1971) **102 n. 39**

Josephus, *Works*, with a translation by H. St J. Thackeray *et al.*, 9 vols. (Loeb Classical Library, Cambridge, Mass. and London, 1926–65) **95 n. 12**

Kelly, J. N. D., *Jerome* (London, 1975) **100 n. 9**

Kittel, R., *Geschichte des Volkes Israel*, 2nd edn (Gotha, 1912) **110 n. 9, 111 n. 26**

Koehler, L., 'Zum Ortsnamen Ezion-Geber', *ZDPV* 59 (1936), 193–5 **98 n. 17, 117 n. 30**

Koenig, J., 'La localisation du Sinai et les traditions des scribes', *Revue d'histoire et de philosophie religieuses* 43 (1963), 2–31, and 44 (1964), 200–35 **87–9, 109 n. 9**

'Itinéraires sinaïtiques en Arabie', *RHR* 166 (1964), 121–41 **87–9, 116 n. 21, 118 n. 46**

Le site de al-Jaw dans l'ancien pays de Madian (Paris, 1971) **87–9, 118 n. 38, n. 39**

Lagrange, M. J., 'Chronique II: Le Sinai', *RB* 6 (1897), 107–30 **104 n. 78**

'Le Sinai biblique', *RB* 8 (1899), 369–92 **103 n. 71, 109 n. 5**

'L'itinéraire des Israélites du pays de Gessen aux bords du Jourdain', *RB* 9 (1900), 63–86, 273–87, 443–9 **107 n. 1, 115 n. 9, 118 n. 53, 119 n. 56**

Lawrence, T. E., *Seven Pillars of Wisdom* (London, 1939) **89, 118 n. 48**

Lawrence, T. E. and Woolley, C. L., *The Wilderness of Zin*, PEF Annual 3, 1914–15 (London, 1915) **114 n. 5**

Le Déaut, R., *Introduction à la littérature targumique* (Rome, 1966–) **97 n. 6, n. 7**

Lepsius, R., *A Tour from Thebes to the Peninsula of Sinai* (ET London, 1846) **109 n. 6**

Briefe aus Aegypten (Berlin, 1852) **109 n. 6**

Le Strange, G., *Palestine under the Moslems* (repr. Beirut, 1965: original edn 1890) **49, 106–7 *passim***

Lewis, A. S., *The Forty Martyrs of the Sinai Desert and the Story of Eulogius*, Horae Semiticae 9 (Cambridge, 1912) **103 n. 49**

Lewy, J., 'The Late Assyro-Babylonian Cult of the Moon and its Culmination at the Time of Nabonidus', *HUCA* 19 (1945–6), 405–89 **109 n. 7**

Lucas, A., *The Route of the Exodus* (London, 1938) **109 n. 8**

McNamara, M., *Targum and Testament* (Shannon, 1972) **96 n. 2**

Marmardji, A. S., *Textes géographiques arabes sur la Palestine*, Études Bibliques (Paris, 1951) **49, 106–7 *passim***

Mekhilta deRabbi Ishmael, ed. H. S. Horowitz, 2nd edn (Jerusalem, 1960) **96 n. 1, 98 n. 20, 99 n. 34, n. 35, n. 38, n. 39**

Meshel, Z., 'History of the Negev in the Time of the Kings of Judah', (unpublished Ph.D. dissertation, Tel Aviv University, 1974) (Heb.) **108 n. 11, 111 n. 20, 117 n. 31**

'Notes and News: Yotvata', *IEJ* 24 (1974), 273–4   **119 n. 63**

'Kuntilat Ajrud – an Israelite Site on the Sinai Border', *Qadmoniot* 9 (1976), 119–24 (Heb.)   **114 n. 7**

'The Name of God in the Wilderness of Zin', *BA* 39 (1976), 6–10   **114 n. 7**

Meshel, Z., and Tsafrir, Y., 'The Nabataean Road from Avdat to Sha'ar Ramon', *PEQ* 106 (1974), 103–18 and 107 (1975), 3–21   **114 n. 8**

Meyer, E., *Die Israeliten und ihre Nachbarstämme* (Halle, 1906)   **109 n. 7, 117 n. 23**

Mian, F., 'L'Anonimo Piacentino al Sinai', *VetChr* 9 (1972), 267–301   **105 n. 84**

Midrash Sifre on Numbers, tr. P. P. Levertoff (London, 1926)   **98 n. 24**

Miller, K., *Mappae Arabicae* (Stuttgart, 1926–31)   **106 n. 8**

Die Peutingersche Tafel (Stuttgart, 1929: repr. 1962)   **105 n. 95, n. 96**

Montgomery, J. A., 'Hebraica: (2) *yam sûp* ("the Red Sea") = *Ultimum Mare?*', *JAOS* 58 (1938), 131–2   **112 n. 42, 113 n. 55**

Moritz, B., *Der Sinaikult in heidnischer Zeit* (Berlin, 1916)   **110 n. 13**

Mowinckel, S., *Psalmenstudien II* (Oslo, 1922)   **110 n. 9**

Musil, A., *The Northern Hegaz* (New York, 1926) (a preliminary report appeared in *Anzeiger der kaiserlichen Akademie der Wissenschaften in Wien, Phil.-hist. Klasse* vol. 48, 139–59 (May, 1911) and was published separately as *Im nördlichen Hejaz* (Vienna, 1911))   **89, 106 n. 2, 109 n. 8, 113 n. 56, 118 n. 47**

Naville, E., *The Store-City of Pithom and the Route of the Exodus* (London, 1885) **94 n. 3 (ch. 2)**

The Route of the Exodus (London, 1891)   **115 n. 9**

Negev, A., *The Inscriptions of Wadi Haggag*, Qedem Monographs, vol. 6 (Jerusalem, 1977)   **97 n. 5, 104 n. 75, n. 77, 105 n. 84, 114 n. 11**

Nielsen, D., 'The Site of the Biblical Mount Sinai', *JPOS* 7 (1927), 187–208 (also published separately (Copenhagen, 1928))   **109 n. 8**

Norin, S., *Er Spaltete das Meer* (Lund, 1977)   **115 n. 7**

Noth, M., 'Die Geschichte des Namens Palästina', *ZDPV* 62 (1939), 125–44   **99 n. 4**

'Der Wallfahrtsweg zum Sinai', *PJB* 36 (1940), 5–28   **60, 87–8, 90, 108 n. 10, 109 n. 3, 118 n. 42, n. 52, n. 53**

'Der Schauplatz des Meereswunders', *Festschrift für O. Eissfeldt*, ed. J. Fueck (Halle, 1947), 181–90   **71, 72, 107 n. 2, 112 n. 45, 115 n. 7**

Überlieferungsgeschichte des Pentateuch (Stuttgart, 1948)   **69, 111 n. 29, n. 34, 112 n. 35, n. 36**

Josua, 2nd edn (Tübingen, 1953)   **118 n. 52**

The History of Israel, 2nd English edn (London, 1960), Gn edn *Geschichte Israels* (Göttingen, 1950) **110 n. 11, 111 n. 24**

Exodus (ET London, 1962), Gn edn *Das zweite Buch Mose* (Göttingen, 1959) **111 n. 33**

Notitia Dignitatum, ed. O. Seeck (Berlin, 1876) **101 n. 34, 118 n. 50**

Oberhummer, E., 'Die Sinaifrage', *Mitteilungen der KK. Geog. Gesellschaft in Wien* 54 (1911), 628–41 (ET in *Annual Report of the Smithsonian Institution, 1912* (Washington, 1913), 669–77) **107 n. 1**

O'Callaghan, R. T., 'Madaba (Carte de) ', *DBS* vol. 5, 627–704 **105 n. 92**

Onomastica Sacra, ed. P. de Lagarde, 2nd edn (Göttingen, 1887: repr. Hildesheim, 1966) **98 n. 18, 99 n. 6, 100–2 passim**

Oren, E., '"Migdol" Fortress in North-Western Sinai', *Qadmoniot* 10 (1977), 71–6 (Heb.) **115 n. 13**

Palmer, E. H., *The Desert of the Exodus* (Cambridge, 1871) **74, 106 n. 3, 107 n. 22, 109 n. 5, 113 n. 56, 118 n. 37, n. 51, 119 n. 57, n. 59**

Parr, P. J., Harding, G. L., and Dayton, J. E., 'Preliminary Survey in North-West Arabia, 1968', *Bulletin of the Institute of Archaeology, University of London* 8–9 (1968–9), 193–242 **110 n. 19**

Perlitt, L., 'Sinai und Horeb', in *Beiträge zur Alttestamentlichen Theologie (Festschrift W. Zimmerli)*, ed. H. Donner, R. Hanhart and R. Smend (Göttingen, 1977), pp. 302–22 **111 n. 33**

Petrie, W. M. F., *Researches in Sinai* (London, 1906) **109 n. 6**

Philby, H. St J., *The Land of Midian* (London, 1957) **110 n. 9**

Phythian-Adams, W. J., 'The Mount of God', *PEFQS* 62 (1930), 135–49 and 192–209 **109 n. 7**

The Call of Israel (Oxford, 1934) **113 n. 56, 117 n. 23**

Pirenne, J., 'Le site préislamique de al-Jaw, la Bible, le Coran, et le Midrash', *RB* 82 (1975), 35–69 **87, 118 n. 40**

Preisigke, F. *Wörterbuch der griechischen Papyrusurkunden* (Berlin, 1925–31) **95 n. 6**

Robinson, E., *Biblical Researches in Palestine, Mount Sinai and Arabia Petraea*, 3 vols. (London, 1841) **46, 76, 78, 84, 109 n. 5, 111 n. 31, 113 n. 3, 114 n. 8, n. 12, n. 13, 117 n. 24, n. 26, n. 33, 118 n. 36, n. 55**

Rothenberg, B., 'König Salomons Hafen im Roten Meer neu entdeckt', *Das Heilige Land* 97 (1965), 18–28 **74, 86, 113 n. 54, 117 n. 34**

'An Archaeological Survey of South Sinai', *PEQ* 102 (1970), 4–29 **48, 78, 97 n. 5, 100 n. 15, 104 n. 77, 105 n. 97, 113 n. 3, 114 n. 11, 117 n. 34**

Timna: Valley of the Biblical Copper Mines (London, 1972) **108 n. 13, 110 n. 19, 117 n. 34**

Rothenberg, B., and Aharoni, Y., *God's Wilderness* (London, 1961) **97 n. 5, 100 n. 15, 113 n. 38, 117 n. 34, 119 n. 56**

Rowley, H. H., *From Joseph to Joshua* (London, 1950) **110 n. 12**

Saarisalo, A., *Arabic Tradition and Topographical Research*, Studia Orientalia XVII: 3 (Helsinki, 1952) **106 n. 14**

Sachsse, E., 'Die römische Strasse durch die Sinaihalbinsel nach der Peutingerschen Tafel', *ZDPV* 51 (1928), 265–8 **105 n. 96**

Saller, S. J., *The Memorial of Moses on Mount Nebo* (Jerusalem, 1941) **102 n. 43**

Saller, S. J., and Bagatti, B., *The Town of Nebo* (Jerusalem, 1949) **102 n. 43**

Sayce, A. H., *The Early History of the Hebrews* (London, 1897) **109 n. 8**

Schiwietz, S., 'Die Altchristliche Tradition über den Berg Sinai und Kosmas Indikopleustes', *Der Katholik*, 4th series, 38 (1908), 9–30 **102 n. 47, 103 n. 50, 104 n. 80, 105 n. 81, n. 90, 109 n. 6**

Schmid, H., *Mose: Überlieferung und Geschichte*, *BZAW* 110 (Berlin, 1968) **111 n. 34, 112 n. 45, 117 n. 23**

Schwartz, J., 'Le "Cycle de Petoubastis" et les commentaires égyptiens de l'Exode', *BIFAO* 49 (1950), 67–83 **94 n. 4**

Seebass, H., *Mose und Aaron: Sinai und Gottesberg* (Bonn, 1962) **111 n. 34**

Segal, J. B., 'Numerals in the Old Testament', *JSS* 10 (1965), 2–20 **108 n. 8**

Servin, A., 'La tradition judéo-chrétienne de l'Exode', *BIE* 31 (1948–9), 315–55 **94 n. 6, 115 n. 10**

van Seters, J., *The Hyksos: A New Investigation* (New Haven and London, 1966) **96 n. 23**

Shafei, Aly Bei, 'Historical Notes on the Pelusiac Branch, the Red Sea Canal and the Route of the Exodus', *Bulletin de la Société Royale de Géographie d'Égypte* 21 (1946), 231–87 **115 n. 8**

Simons, J., *The Geographical and Topographical Texts of the Old Testament* (Leiden, 1959) **98 n. 19, 112 n. 42, n. 43, n. 51, 113 n. 54, 114 n. 4, 115 n. 4, n. 5, n. 9, 117 n. 25, 119 n. 57**

Skrobucha, H., *Sinai* (ET London, 1966: Gn edn, Olten, 1959) **103 n. 50, n. 51, 105 n. 90**

Smend, R., *Yahweh War and Tribal Confederacy* (ET Nashville and New York, 1970), Gn edn *Jahwekrieg und Stämmebund* (Göttingen, 1963) **111 n. 34**

Smith, George Adam, *The Historical Geography of the Holy Land*, 25th edn (London, 1931: repr. 1966) **107 n. 27, 114 n. 7, 117 n. 30, 119 n. 60**

Snaith, N. H., 'יַם סוּף: the Sea of Reeds: the Red Sea', *VT* 15 (1965), 395–8 **112 n. 37, n. 42, n. 49**

Stanley, A. P., *Sinai and Palestine* (London, 1858) **112 n. 40, 118 n. 55**

Swete, H. B., *Introduction to the Old Testament in Greek*, 2nd edn (Cambridge, 1902) **95 n. 14**

Thomsen, P., 'Untersuchungen zur älteren Palästina-literatur', *ZDPV* 29 (1906), 101–32 **114 n. 8**

Loca Sancta (Leipzig, 1907: repr. Hildesheim, 1966) **101 n. 29, n. 32, n. 37, 102 n. 39, n. 45**

'Die römischen Meilensteine der Provinzen Syria, Arabia und Palästina', *ZDPV* 40 (1917), 1–103 **102 n. 39**

Thomson, J. O., *History of Ancient Geography*, (Cambridge, 1948) **105 n. 95**

Trumbull, H. Clay, *Kadesh–Barnea* (London, 1884) **74, 108 n. 6, 112 n. 40, n. 41, 113 n. 56, n. 57, n. 58, 118 n. 36, 119 n. 56**

Tsafrir, Y., 'Monks and Monasteries in Southern Sinai', *Qadmoniot* 3 (1970), 2–18 (Heb.) **98 n. 28, 100 n. 23, 103 n. 51**

Uphill, E. L., 'Pithom and Raamses: their Location and Significance', *JNES* 27 (1968), 281–316 and 28 (1969), 15–39 **114 n. 2, n. 3**

de Vaulx, J., *Les Nombres*, Sources Bibliques (Paris, 1972) **94 n. 5**

de Vaux, R., *Histoire ancienne d'Israel*, vol. 1, Études Bibliques (Paris, 1971) **88, 107 n. 1, 108 n. 14, 110 n. 14, 111 n. 20, 113 n. 55, 118 n. 44, n. 50, n. 54**

Vestri, L., 'Considerazioni sull'itinerario dell'Esodo: la tappa di Obot', *Bibbia e Oriente* 6 (1964), 86–93 **118 n. 53**

Ward, W. A., 'The Semitic Biconsonantal Root *sp* and the Common Origin of Egyptian *čwf* and Hebrew *sûp* = " Marsh (-Plant) " ', *VT* 24 (1974), 339–49 **112 n. 43, n. 47, 113 n. 55**

Waterhouse, S. D., and Ibach, R., 'Heshbon 1973: the Topographical Survey', *AUSS* 13 (1975), 217–33 **102 n. 39, n. 46**

Weippert, M., Review of R. Giveon, *Les bédouins shosou...*, *Biblica* 35 (1974), 265–80, 427–33 **108 n. 4**

Wellhausen, J., *Prolegomena to the History of Israel* (ET Edinburgh, 1885: repr. New York, 1957), Gn edn *Prolegomena zur Geschichte Israels* (Berlin, 1883) **67, 109 n. 8, 111 n. 27**

Wiegand, T., *Sinai* (Berlin and Leipzig, 1920) **110 n. 9**

Wilkinson, J., *Egeria's Travels* (London, 1971) **98 n. 26, 99 n. 8, 103–4 *passim*, 105 n. 83**

'L'apport de Saint Jérôme à la topographie', *RB* 81 (1974), 245–57 **100 n. 9**

Wilson, J. A., 'Buto and Hierakonpolis in the Geography of Egypt', *JNES* 14 (1955), 209–36 **114 n. 6**

Winnett, F. V., *The Mosaic Tradition* (Toronto, 1949) **112 n. 42, 113 n. 55, 116 n. 20**

Winstedt, E. O., 'Notes on the MSS. of Cosmas Indicopleustes', *JTS* 8 (1907), 607–14 **104 n. 80**

Winton Thomas, D. (ed.), *Archaeology and Old Testament Study* (Oxford, 1967) **108 n. 11**

Wissmann, H. von, 'Madiama', *RE*, supp. vol. 12, cols. 525–52 **106 n. 2, 109 n. 9, 110 n. 17**

de Wit, C., *The Date and Route of the Exodus* (London, 1960) **107 n. 1**

Wolf, C. U., 'Eusebius of Caesarea and the Onomasticon ', *BA* 27 (1964), 66–96 **100 n. 9**

Wolska (-Conus), W., *La topographie chrétienne de Cosmas Indicopleustès* (Paris, 1962) **104 n. 76**

(ed.), *Cosmas Indicopleustès, Topographie chrétienne*, 3 vols., *SC* 141 (1968), 159 (1970) and 197 (1973) **104 n. 76, n. 78**

Wright, G. E., *Biblical Archaeology* (London, 1962) **115 n. 8**

Zuber, B., *Vier Studien zu den Ursprüngen Israels*, Orbis Biblicus et Orientalis 9 (Freiburg, 1976) **88, 109 n. 9, 111 n. 25, n. 26, 118 n. 41, n. 45**

van Zyl, A. H., *The Moabites* (Leiden, 1960) **119 n. 58**

GENERAL INDEX

INDEX OF BIBLICAL REFERENCES

OLD TESTAMENT

Gen. 1: 10   **112 n. 50**
    14: 6   **100 n. 18**
    15: 18   **26**
    16: 7   **77**
    16: 14   **74**
    20: 1   **74**
    21: 21   **100 n. 18**
    33: 17   **27, 79**
    41: 50–2   **8**
    45: 10   **5, 8**
    46: 28   **5**
    46: 28–9   **6, 8**
    46: 29   **5**
    46: 34   **5**
    47: 11   **5**
    47: 27   **95 n. 15**

Ex. 1: 11   **8, 20, 22, 79, 94 n. 4 (ch. 2)**
    2: 3   **28, 70–1**
    2: 5   **71**
    2: 15   **33**
    2: 22   **95 n. 14**
    3: 1   **65, 68, 111 n. 33**
    3: 12   **68**
    3: 18   **67–8**
    4: 27   **68**
    5: 3   **67**
    6: 15   **95 n. 9**
    8: 23   **67**
    10: 9   **68**
    10: 19   **71**
    12: 37   **1, 27, 94 n. 2 (ch. 1)**
    13: 17–18   **7, 13, 116 n. 20**
    13: 18   **6, 28, 70, 83**
    13: 20   **94 n. 2 (ch. 1)**
    14   **9, 72**
    14: 2   **5, 27, 81–2, 94 n. 2 (ch. 1), 98 n. 20**
    14: 9   **5, 94 n. 2 (ch. 1)**
    14: 11–12   **83**
    15–17   **66**
    15–18   **67**

15: 4   **6, 72–3**
15: 22   **6, 18–19, 60, 72, 80, 94 n. 2 (ch. 1), 99 n. 34**
15: 23   **6, 94 n. 2 (ch. 1)**
15: 23–6   **67**
15: 27   **94 n. 2 (ch. 1)**
16: 1   **94 n. 2 (ch. 1)**
16: 13   **68**
17: 1   **94 n. 2 (ch. 1)**
17: 1–7   **43, 45, 67**
17: 7   **6, 14**
17: 8–13   **7**
17: 8–16   **111 n. 28**
18   **69**
19   **111 n. 21**
19: 1   **68, 94 n. 2 (ch. 1), 114 n. 1**
19: 2   **27, 94 n. 2 (ch. 1)**
19: 4   **27**
19: 18   **65**
23: 31   **112 n. 44**

Num. 10   **23**
10: 11   **68**
10: 12   **23, 94 n. 2 (ch. 1), 114 n. 1**
10: 30   **65**
10: 33   **23–4, 60, 94 n. 2 (ch. 1)**
11   **67**
11: 3   **14**
11: 34   **14, 108 n. 9**
11: 35   **94 n. 2 (ch. 1), 108 n. 9**
12: 16   **94 n. 2 (ch. 1)**
13: 3   **42, 91**
13: 21   **91**
13: 26   **4, 42**
14: 25   **42**
14: 32   **15**
20   **67**
20: 1   **17, 94 n. 2 (ch. 1), 96 n. 19, 114 n. 1**
20: 2–13   **54**
20: 11   **17**

NEW TESTAMENT